How to Needle Felt

Christmas Ornaments

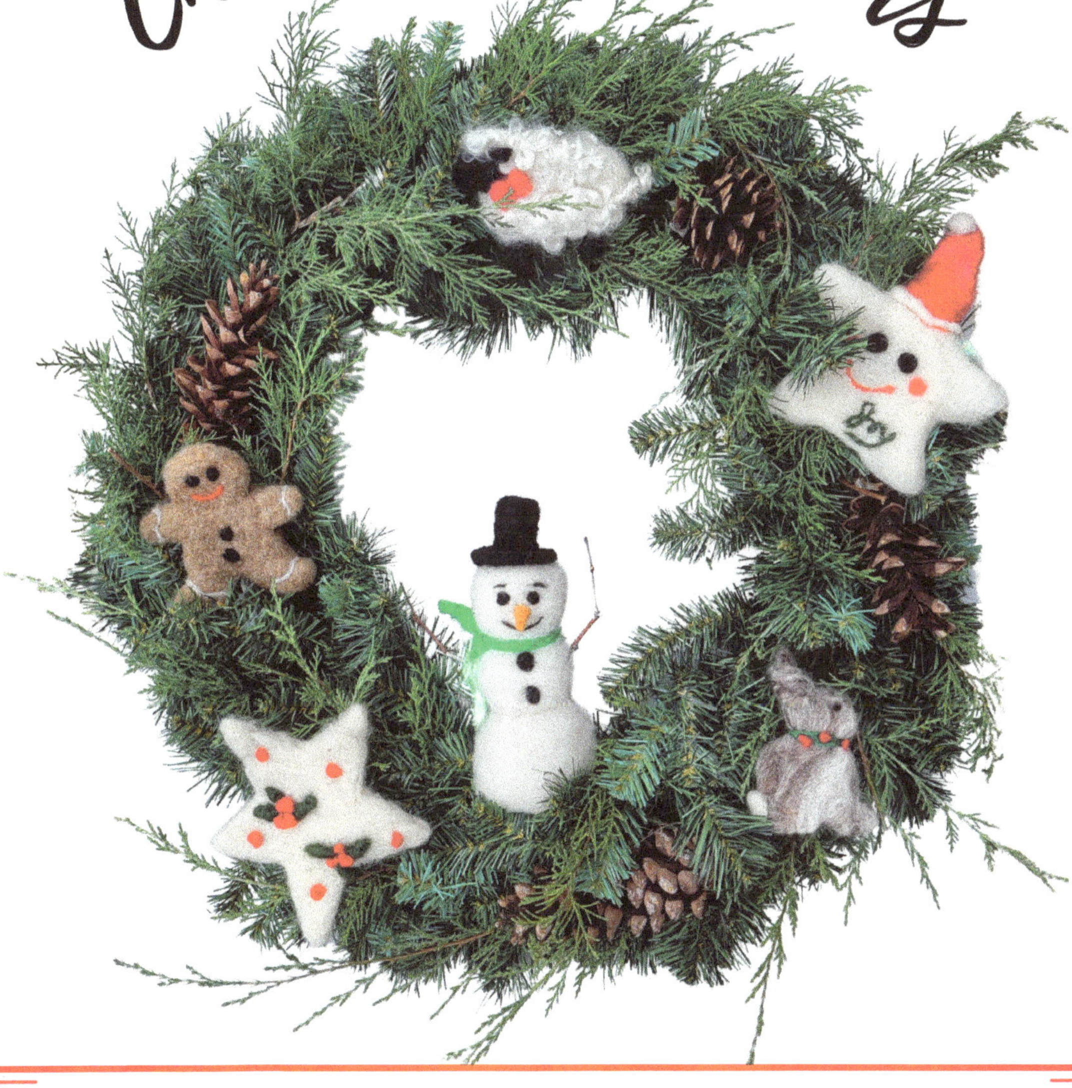

14 Easy, Fast Wool Projects for Beginners!

By Lori Rea

@NatureCrafty

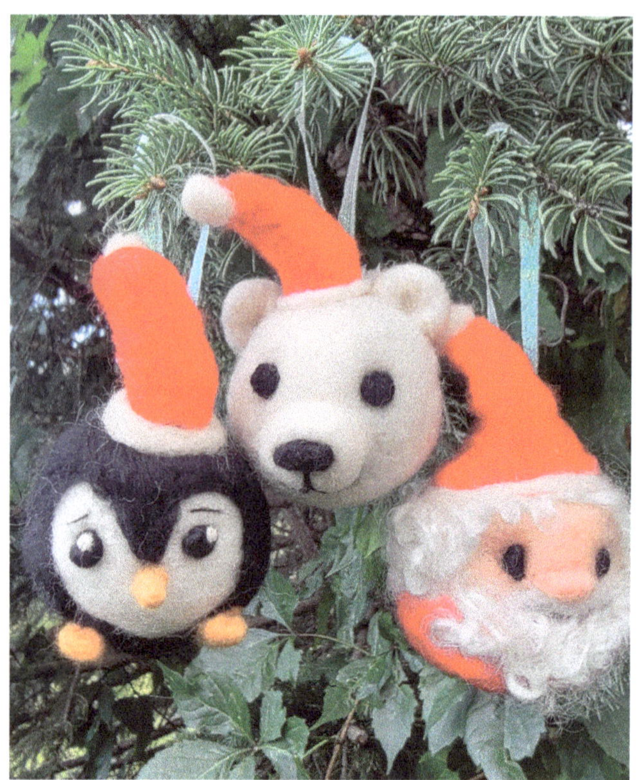
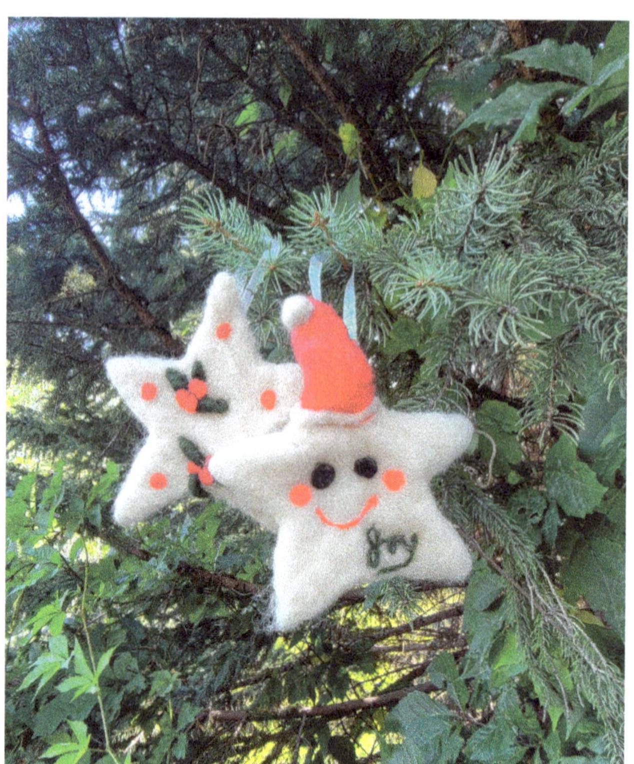
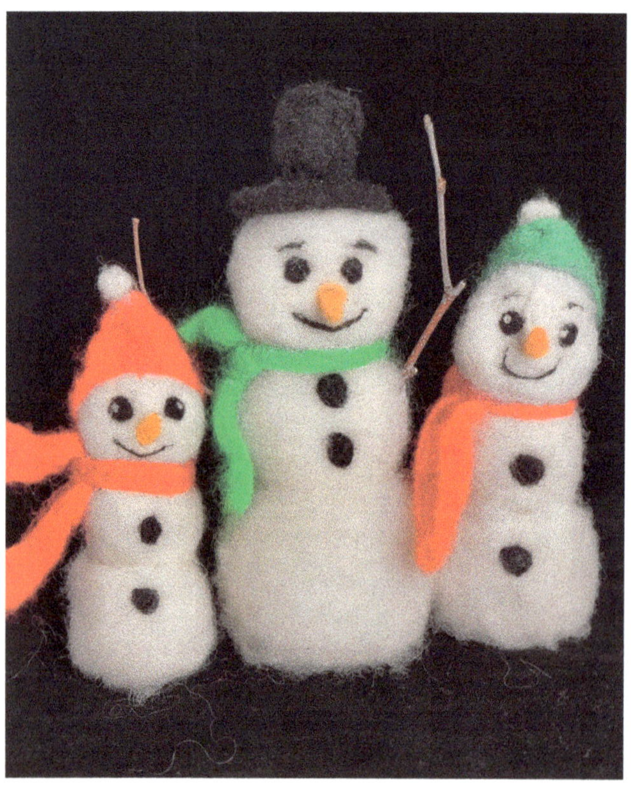
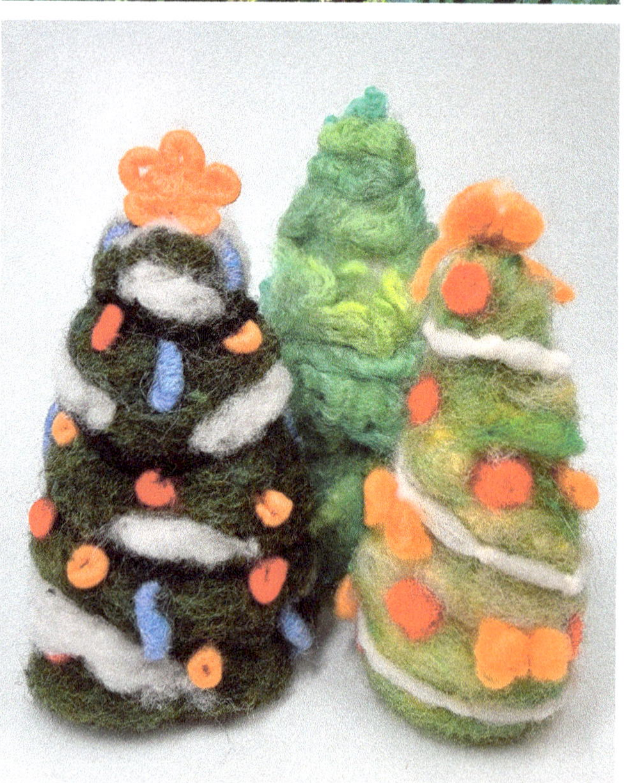

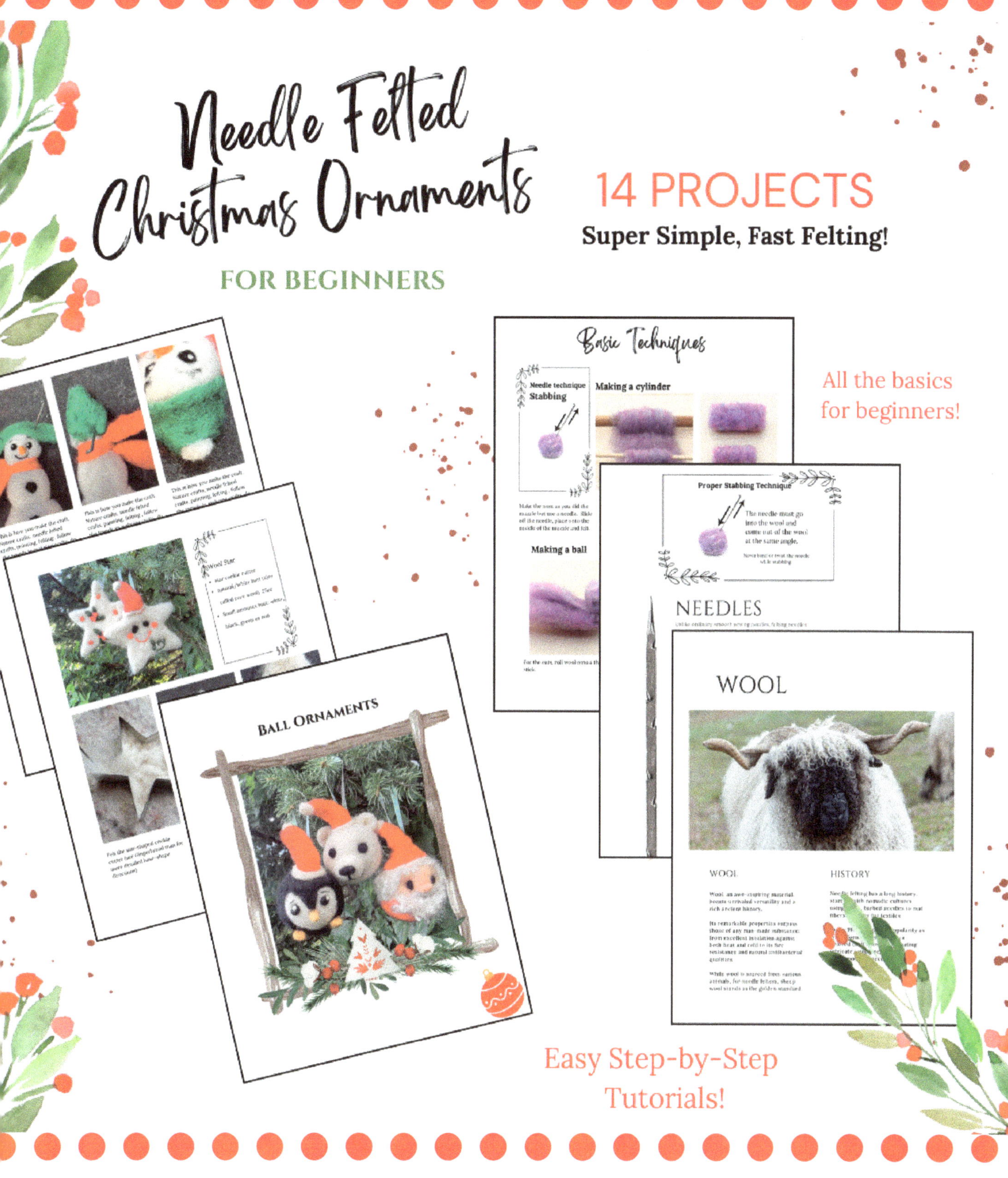

Needle Felted
Christmas Ornaments
FOR BEGINNERS

14 PROJECTS
Super Simple, Fast Felting!

All the basics
for beginners!

Easy Step-by-Step
Tutorials!

Basic Techniques
Needle technique
Stabbing
Making a cylinder
Making a ball

Proper Stabbing Technique
The needle must go
into the wool and
come out of the wool
at the same angle.

NEEDLES

WOOL
WOOL
HISTORY

BALL ORNAMENTS

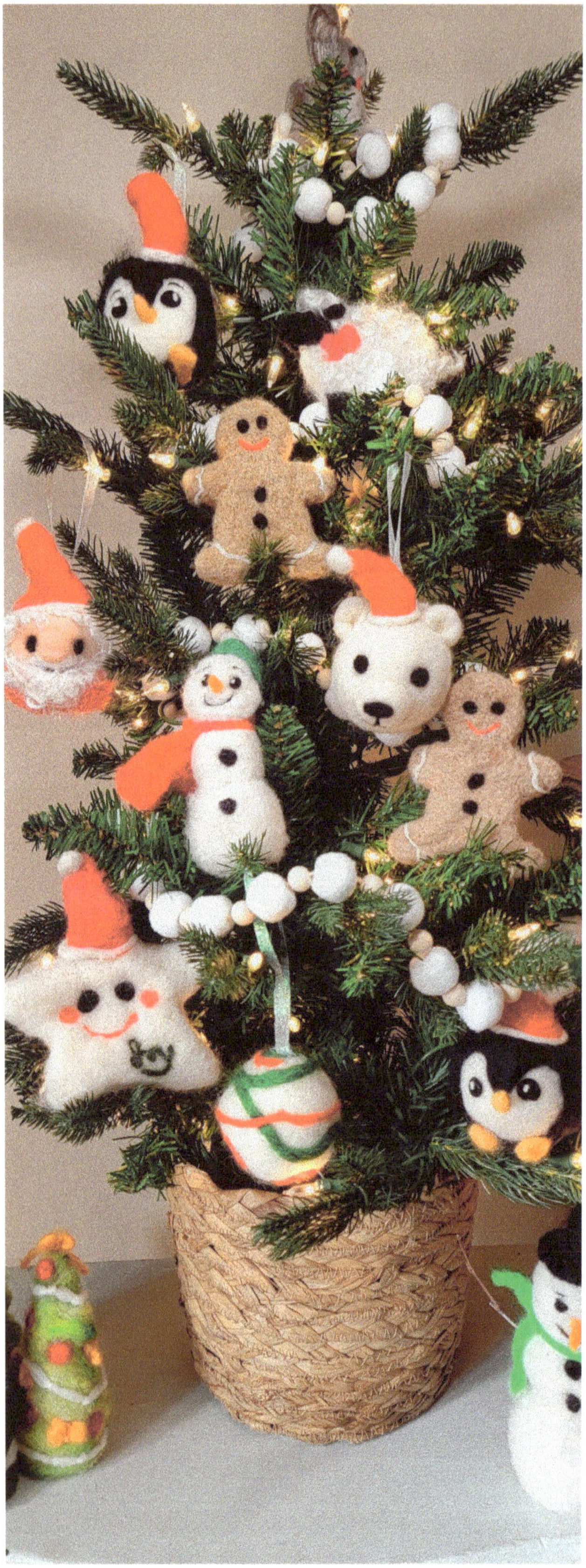

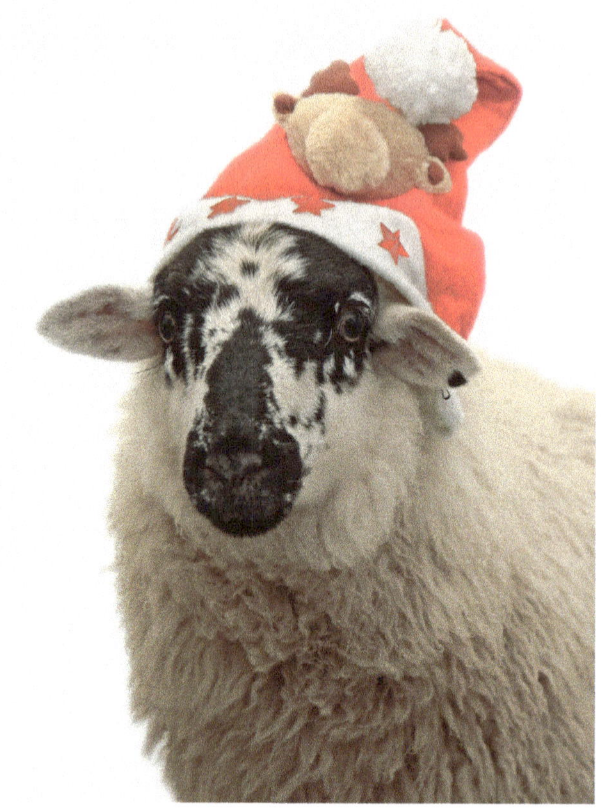

Copyright page

First published in the USA by
NatureCraft Publishing
ISBN: 978-1-7343141-3-7
www.NatureCrafty.com

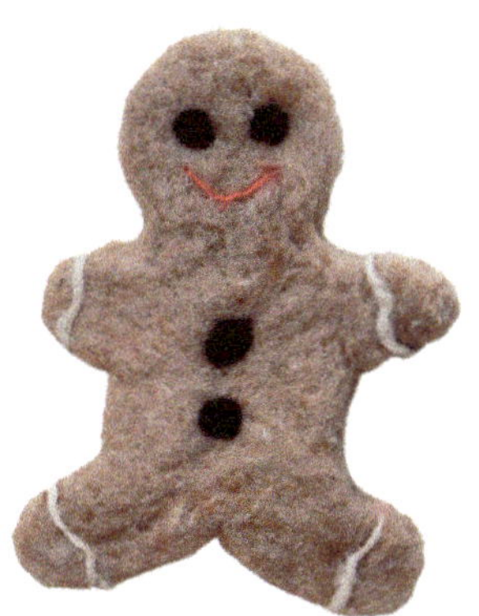

Table of Contents

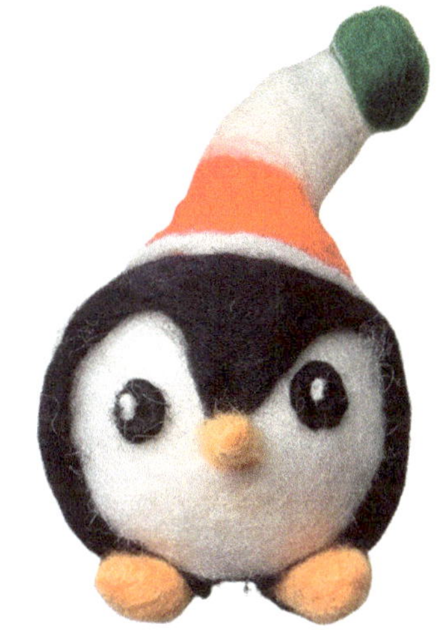

BASICS

PROJECTS

RESOURCES

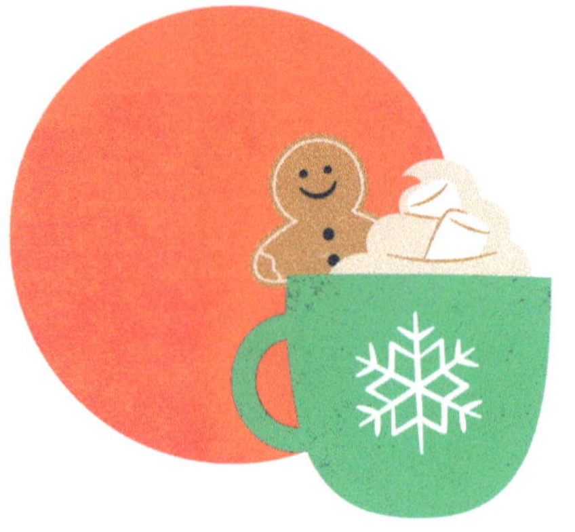

Connect

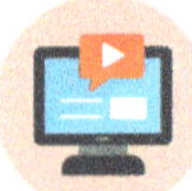
Website: www.NatureCrafty.com

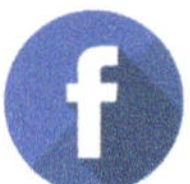
Join our Facebook Group
Group Name: "Needle Felting Made Easy"

@nature.crafty
@creative.felting (see all the new stuff!)

Online Felting Courses:
www.NatureCrafty.com

YouTube: Nature Crafty (video tutorials)

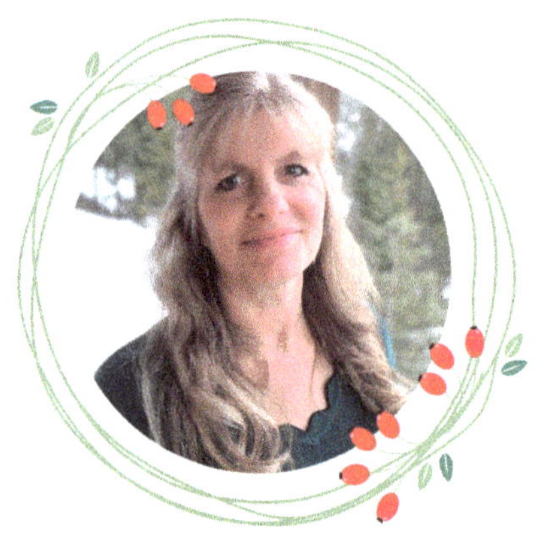

Amazon Books: **Courses Etsy**:
Lori Rea   Creative Felting

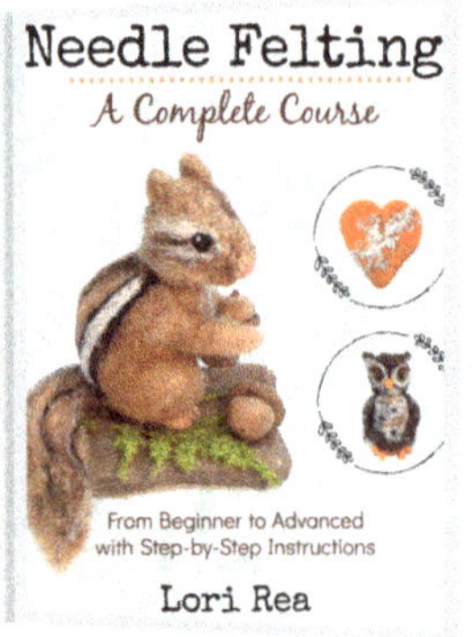

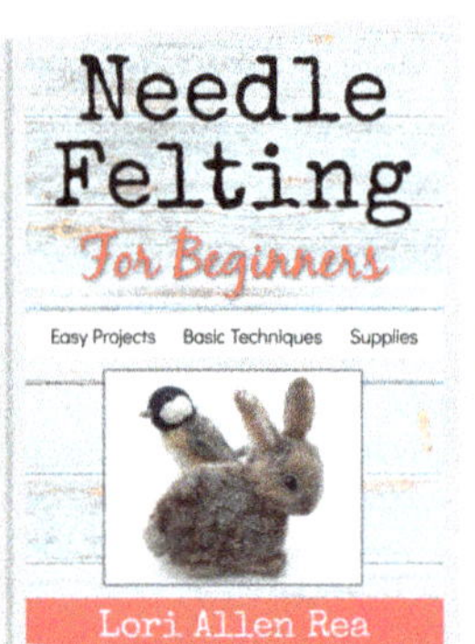

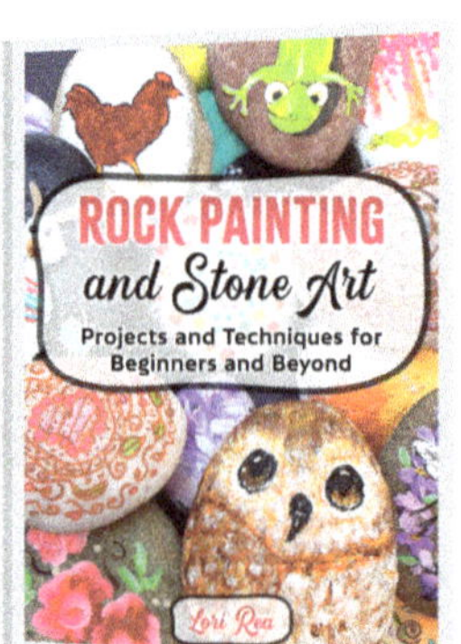

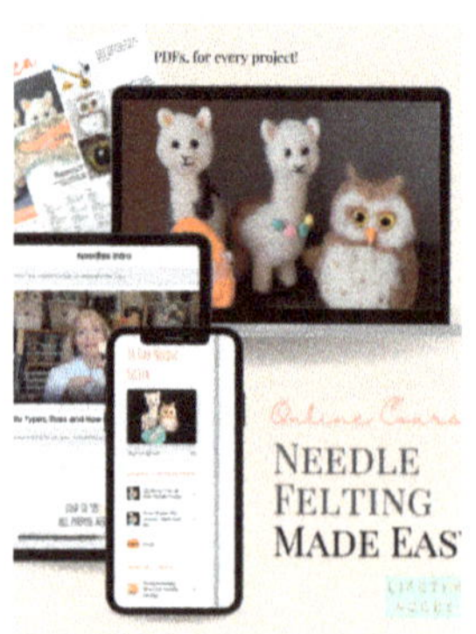

INTRODUCTION

What is Needle Felting?

In its simplest terms, needle felting is the process of turning wool into felt by using a specialized needle.

This sharp, notched needle tangles and locks the wool fibers together as it is stabbed into the wool.

By tightly rolling the wool to remove air and then repeatedly poking it, the scales on the fibers become entangled and matted together.

 It doesn't take much time before a mound of fluffy wool begins to take shape and evolve into a beautiful sculpture.

Why Needle felt?

Sculpting with wool is very therapeutic and gratifying. Many claim the stabbing motion is a great way to unwind and release stress. Needle felting is also an eco-friendly craft that uses natural materials and is easy on the environment.

Needle felting is easy to learn, and it costs very little to get started. The basic supplies are simply wool and needles plus a pad to work on, making this an easy-entry craft.

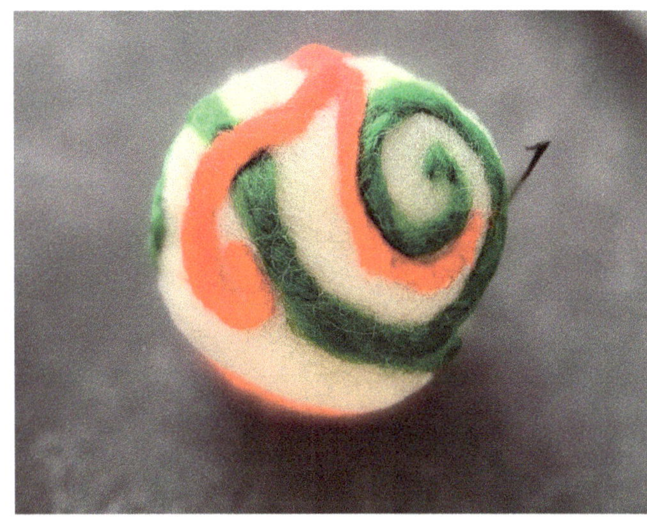

Book Projects

I've designed the ornaments in this book with simplicity in mind, ensuring they're perfect for beginners.

Not only are they a joy to create, but they also make for fantastic group projects with friends.

Additionally, I've purposefully selected projects that are not only easy and fun, but also have great potential for those looking to turn their felting skills into money.

These ornaments are fast to make, particularly as you gain experience, making them a lucrative choice for those interested in selling their creations.

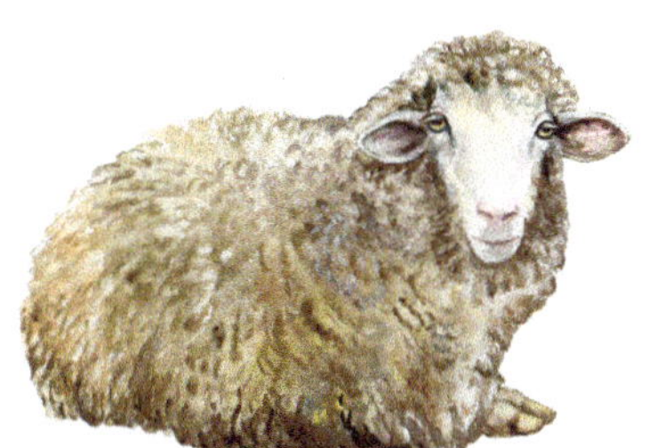

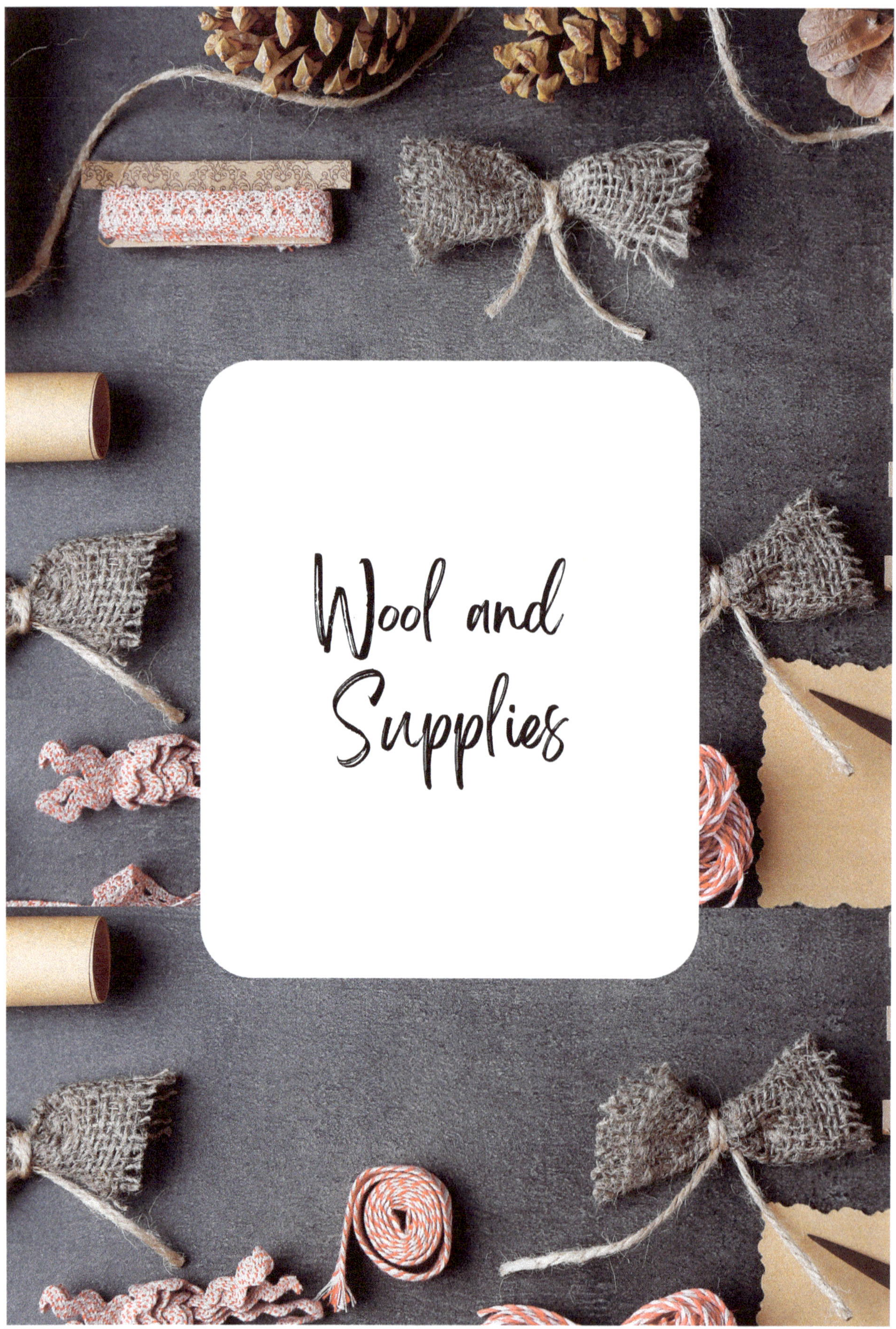

Wool and
Supplies

WOOL

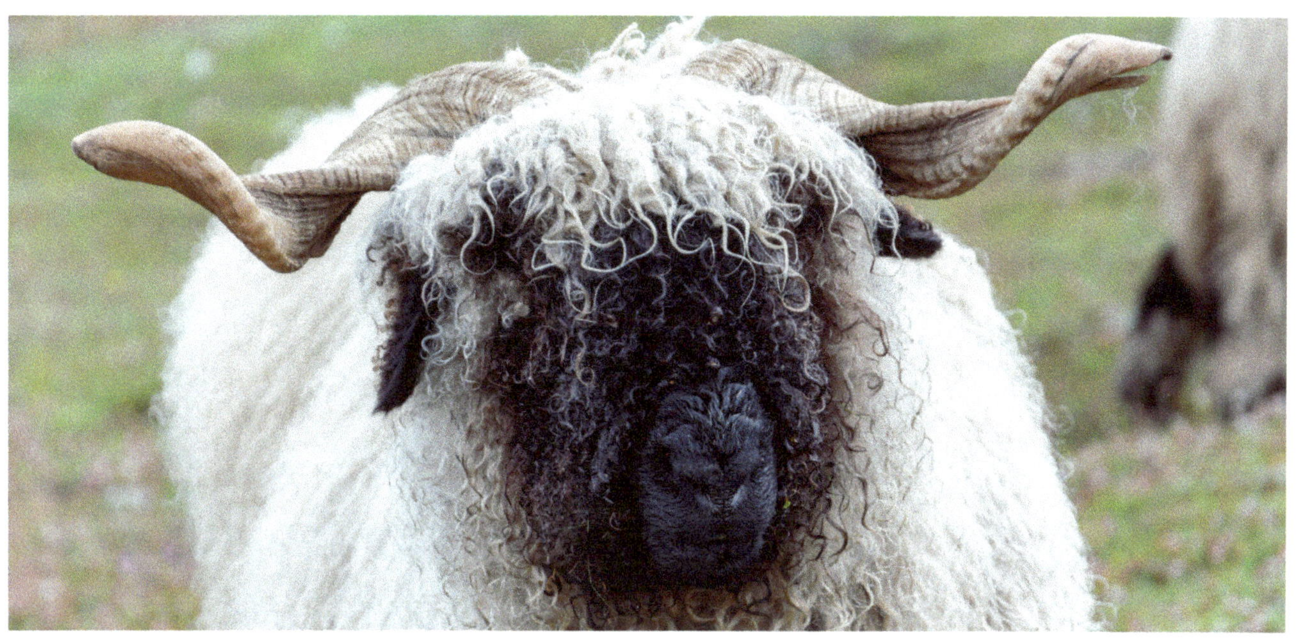

WOOL IS AMAZING!

Wool is a remarkable natural fiber that has been cherished by humans for millennia. Derived from the fleece of sheep and other animals like goats and rabbits, wool has a rich history of utility and innovation.

One of its outstanding characteristics is its exceptional insulation properties. Wool fibers have a unique structure that allows them to trap air effectively, making woolen garments superb insulators against both cold and heat.

This quality has made wool a favorite choice for clothing, from cozy sweaters for winter warmth to lightweight, breathable garments suitable for all seasons.

MORE THAN JUST SHEEP

Although sheep wool is the golden standard for felting, needle felters often utilize various other animal fibers to create unique textures and colors in their projects.

Alpaca and llama wool are popular choices, known for their softness and hypoallergenic properties. Angora rabbit fur offers a fluffy and luxurious feel, while mohair, derived from the Angora goat, provides a distinct sheen.

Fibers like camel, yak, and even dog and cat hair can also be used, although such exotic fibers are generally reserved for the outside or top of projects.

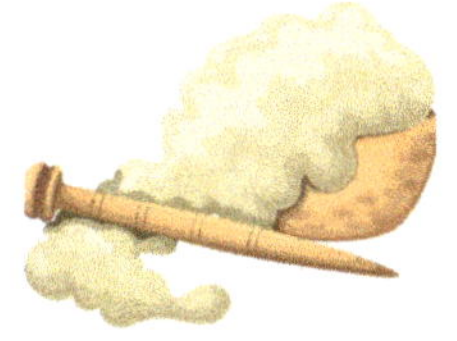

Wool is also eco-friendly, being biodegradable, sustainable, and renewable, making it a timeless and valuable resource in our modern world.

WOOL PRODUCTS

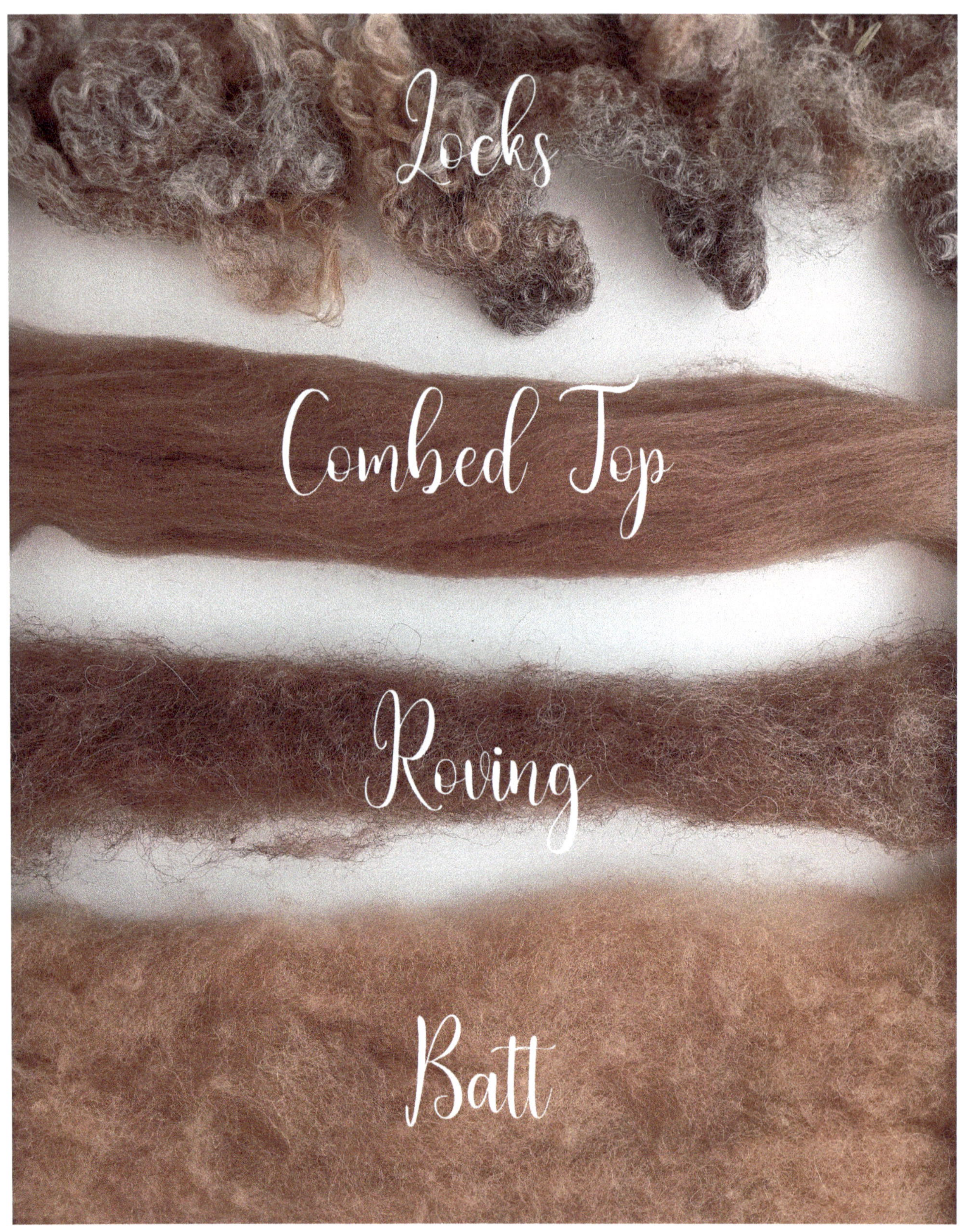

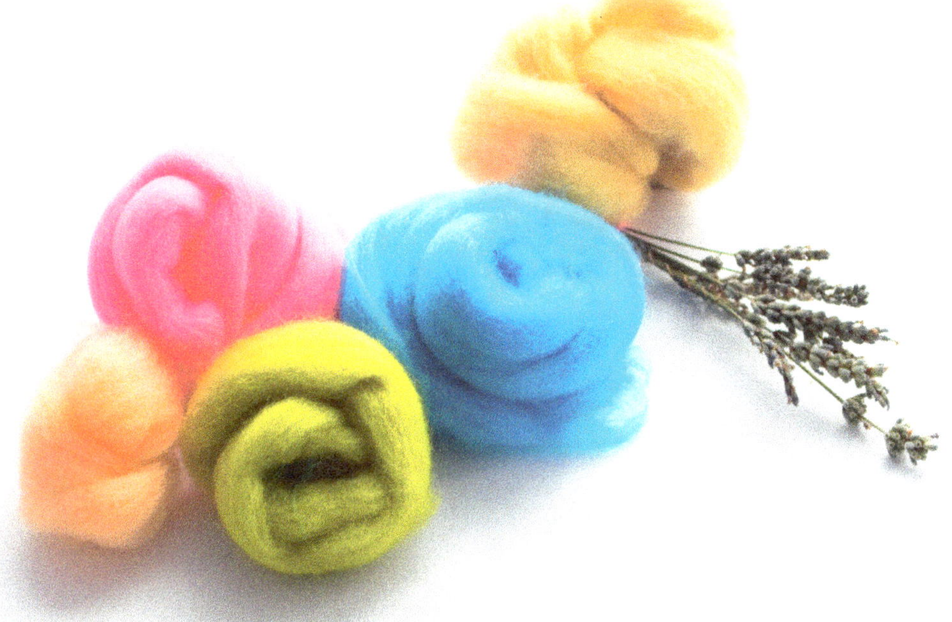

TYPES OF WOOL PRODUCTS

There are four main types of wool fiber products used in needle felting:

- **Batt**: A sheet-like wool product made by blending wool fiber on a machine. Batt is perfect for both core/foundation work or sculpting intricate details. Batt felts up quickly.

- **Roving**: A long bundle of wool fibers, in rope form, with the texture being similar to batt. Ideal for wrapping armatures and core work, its even thickness ensures consistent results and seamless finishes.

- **Top**: Also called combed top, this refined fiber has parallel-aligned fibers, providing a silky appearance. Needle felters use it to produce smooth surfaces, add fine details, blend colors, and achieve a sheen.

- **Locks**: There are various breeds of sheep and goats that produce curly coats. Locks are the uncombed part of the coat that is used in decorative ways such as Santa beards and sheep sculptures.

NEEDLE FELTING TERMS

Needle felting is a unique craft that comes with its own set of terminology. Terms vary by country.

- **Core Wool**: Core wool refers to the foundational wool used in needle felting, providing a sturdy structure with its coarse, dense, and high crimp fibers that interlock when poked with a felting needle. It is a fast-felting fiber product, commonly found in batt or roving forms. Usually less expensive as it is sold in its natural, or undyed state.

- **Finishing Fibers**: These finer fibers, also known as surface fibers, add intricate details and color to the project, enhancing its appearance. Examples of finishing fibers include combed top, which adds sheen and smoothness, locks that introduce curls, and a range of specialty fibers from different animal sources (bison, llama, cat) or plant origins (flax, rose fiber).

- **Top Coat:** This refers to the coat or pelt you would put onto the top of your project, usually an animal.

CHOOSING WOOL

BATT OR ROVING
FOR FAST FELTING/CORE

Fast felting: Choose either a batt (sometimes referred to as core wool) or roving.

Using batt or roving for the core of your project is essential for two reasons: you will save time and money!

Batt and roving products save time because they yield quick results with less time spent poking. They also cost less to use because they have more bulk and don't shrink as much when you felt them. Batts can also be purchased in bulk.

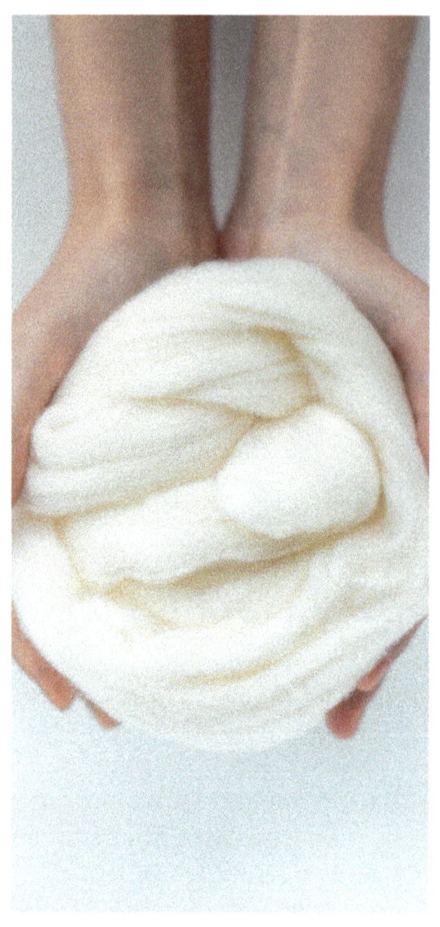

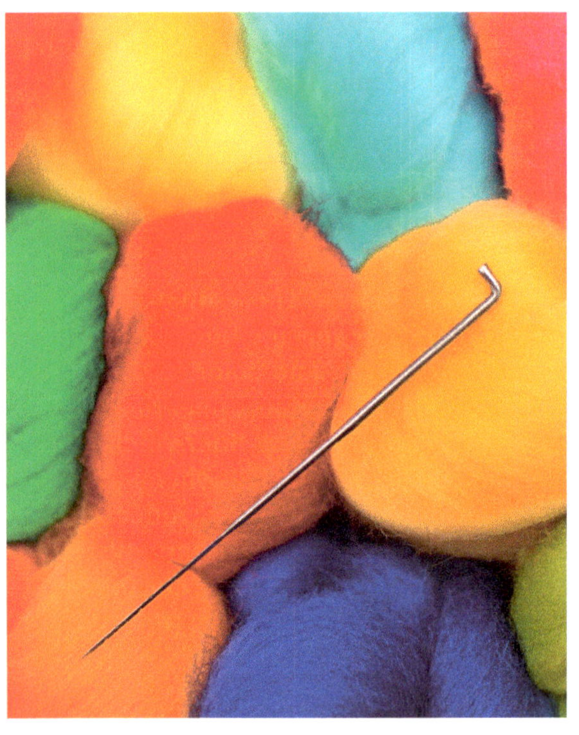

COMBED TOP
FOR SHEEN/COLOR

Finishing details: Combed Top offers a wide range of hues and adds a sleek touch to your project's final appearance.

However, using it to construct the main body of your piece might lead to disappointment. Top requires a significant amount of time to achieve a solid felting.

Use top for delicate lines, smoothness, and shine.

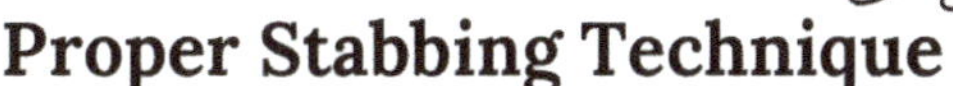

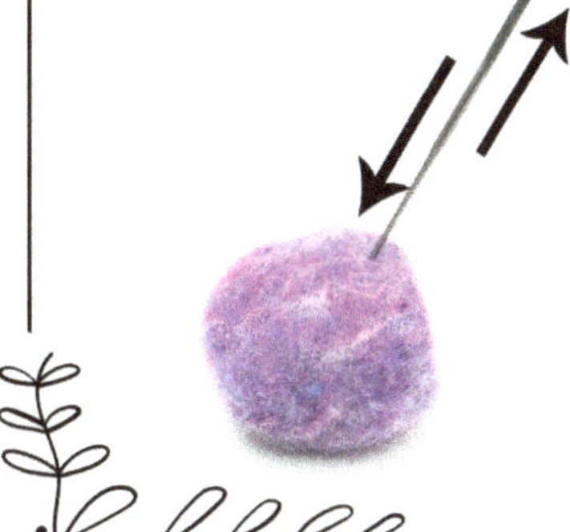

The needle must go into the wool and come out of the wool at the same angle.

Never bend or twist the needle while stabbing.

NEEDLES

Felting needles are different from regular sewing needles. They have small notches cut into their metal shafts which help them catch and tangle fibers when you poke them into wool. This special process is what turns loose wool into a solid and felted material, and it's what makes needle felting an art form.

When choosing felting needles, consider two essential factors: **type and gauge**.

- **Type**: Refers to the needle's style, the number of barbs, and their placement. There are various types available, such as triangle, star, spiral, and reverse.

- **Gauge**: Represents the needle's size. Gauges range from #32 to #42. The higher numbers represent finer needles and the lower the number the thicker the needle.

- The lower numbers (32, 36, 38) are great for fast felting and are larger in size. Use them for the core of the project.

- The higher numbers (40, 42) indicate thinner needles, ideal for finishing touches.

For an all-purpose needle that can do everything, I recommend getting a #38 triangle needle.

TOOLS

Needle holders are handy devices that save on wear and tear on your hands and wrists. It takes less energy to hold an ergonomic tool than a tiny needle.

Needle holders range in capacity from 1 needle up to 12. Holders are optional, you don't have to have one, but they can cut down on felting time and keep you from getting hand fatigue.

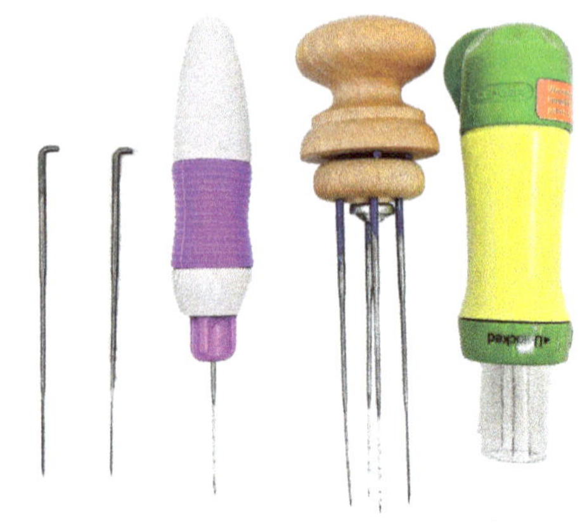

Rolling tools of a variety of types can be used for the projects in this book. Dowel rods, skewers or even pencils can all be used successfully.

The tool that I love the most though, that is specifically made for felters, is the Zullitool by *Sarafina Fiber art. It gives you the ability to tightly roll different widths and sizes.

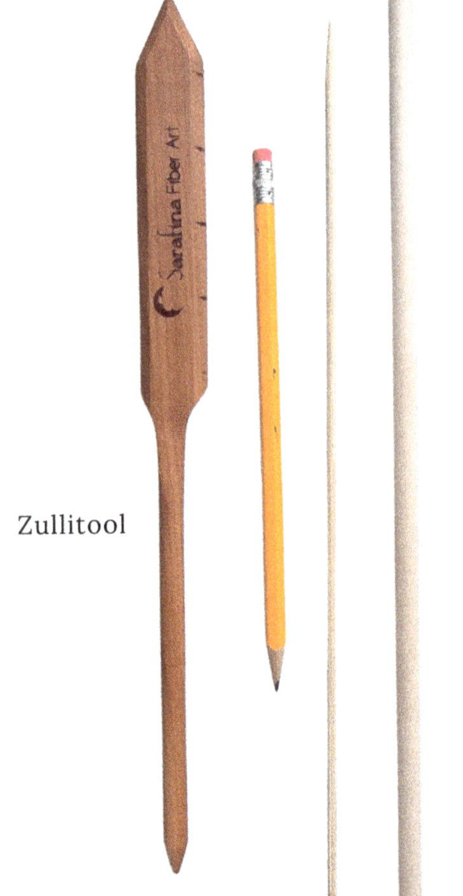

Zullitool

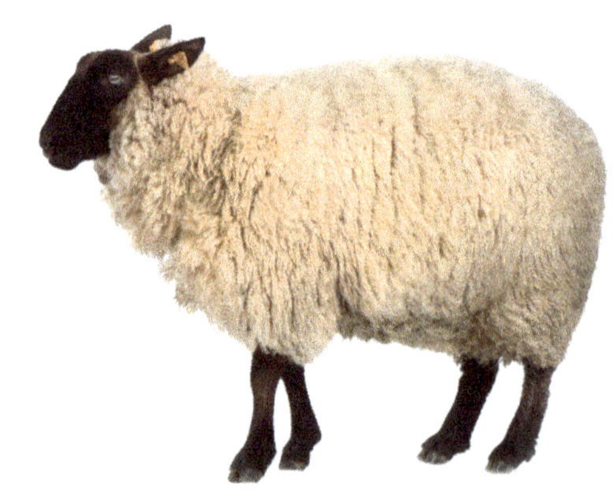

*Go to the Resource section for buying information.

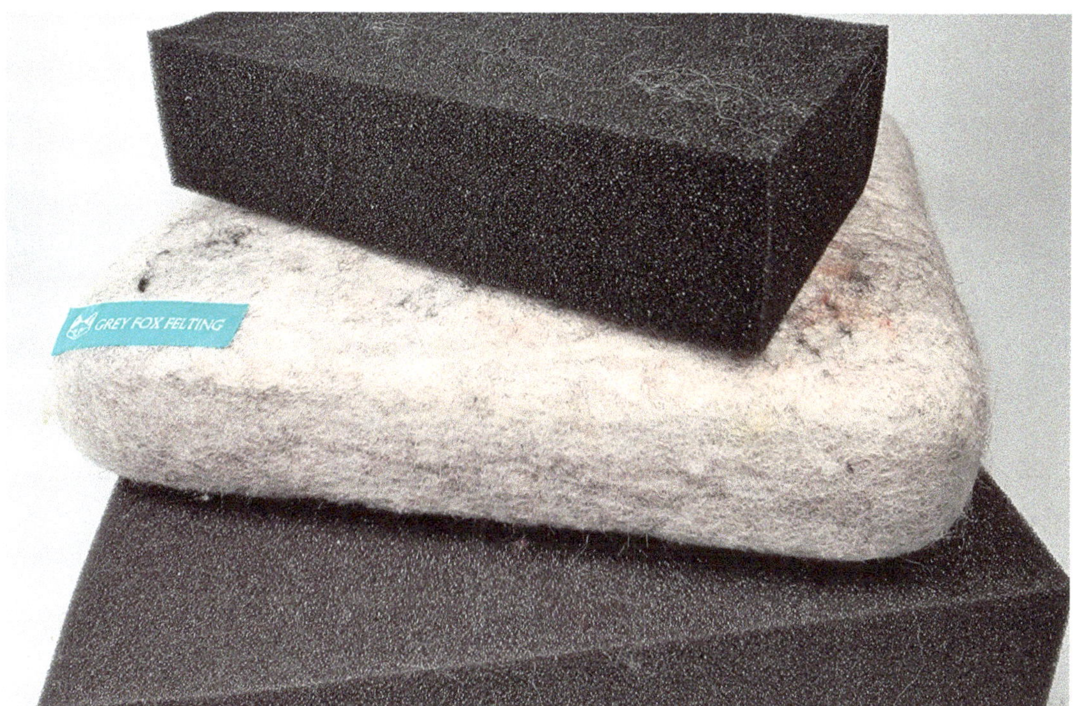

PADS

Felting needles are both sharp and fragile. **To protect you and your work area you will need a firm surface or pad to work on.** There are several types of pads available: foam, brush pads, rice-filled fabric bags and wool mats.

Foam pads are the most popular felting surface. Always buy new foam pads and ask if they are free from chemical fire retardants.

Rice bags are simple and can be made or purchased. Rice-filled bags are an eco-friendly choice.

Wool mats are basically just wool that has been felted together. You might think it's strange to felt on top of wool because you'd expect your project to get stuck, but these mats are tightly felted, so your projects hardly ever stick to them. They are also the most quiet to work on.

Brush pads for needle felting can be found in most major craft stores. Brushes are small and only work for small items.

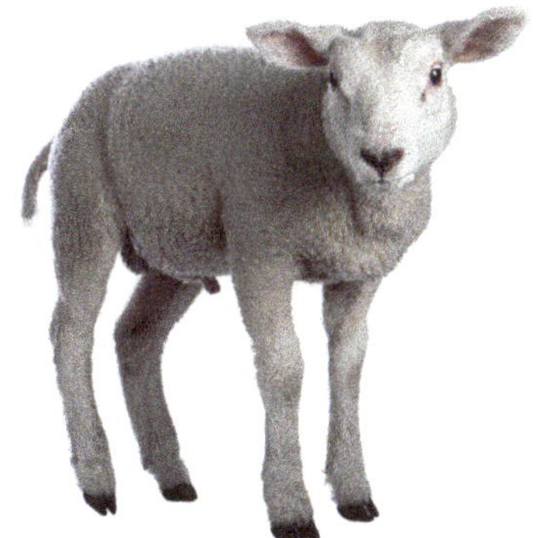

TIP: Never use old upholstery foam that has been labeled as "fire retardant" as these chemicals can be dangerous to inhale as dust is made while stabbing it.

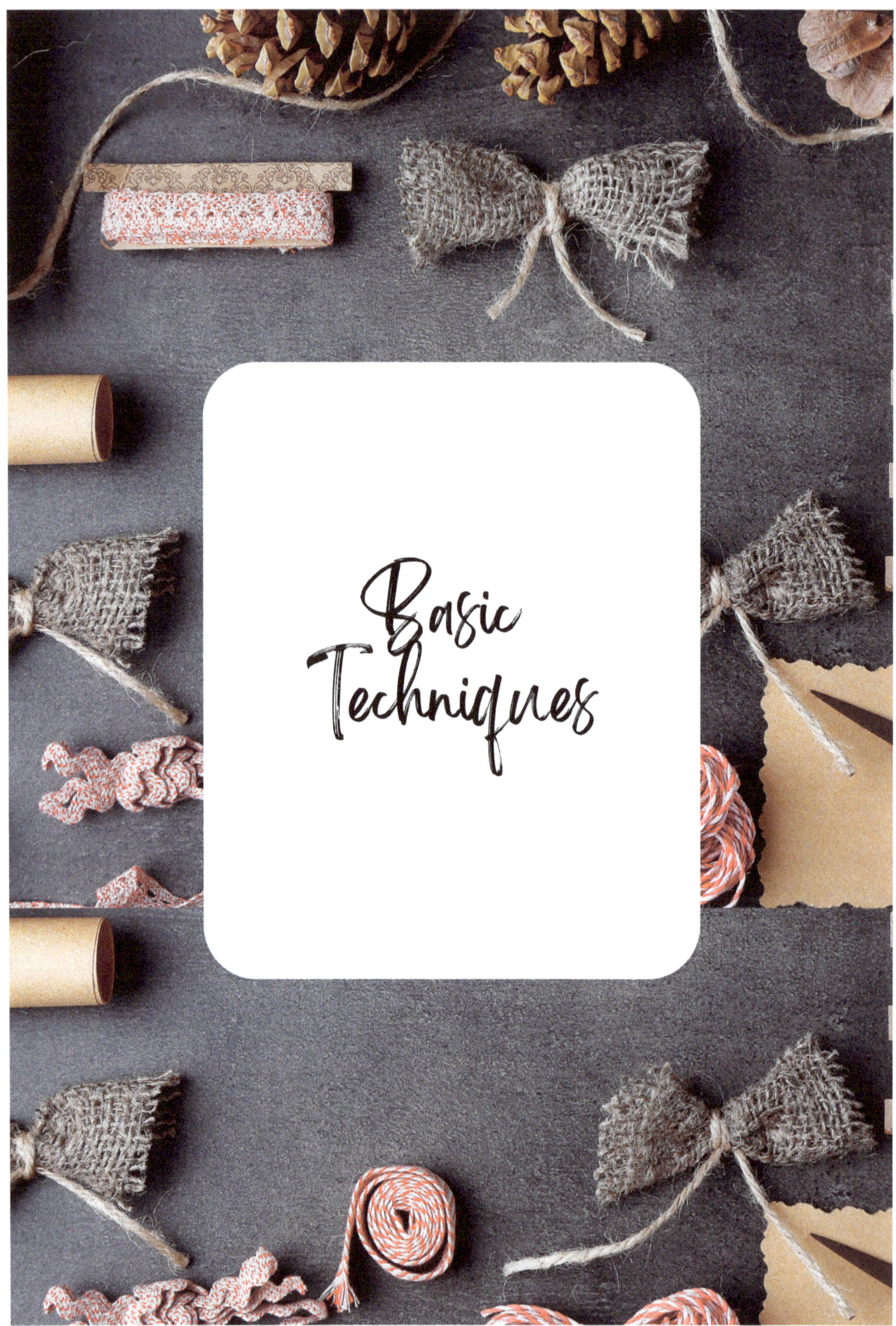

Basic
Techniques

Basic Techniques

How to stab

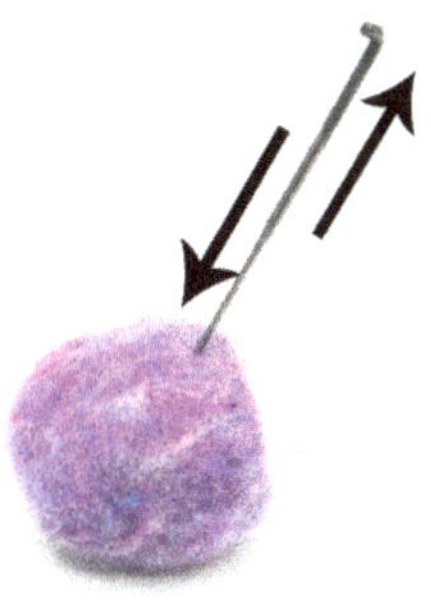

The needle must always go into and come out of the wool at the same angle.

For core work, stab deeply. For finishing work, keep to the top 1/4" of the piece.

Making a cylinder

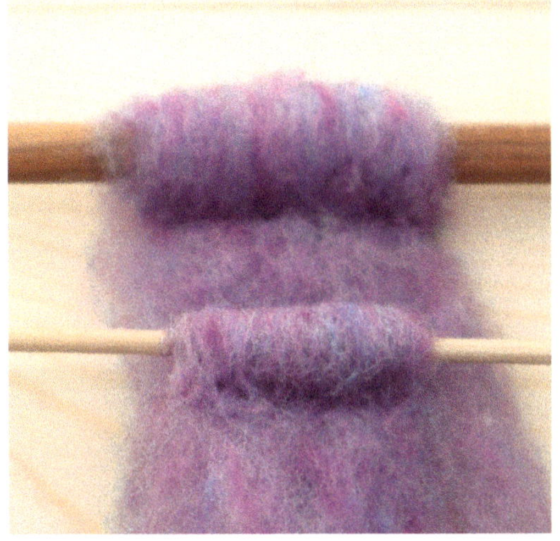

Good, tight cylinders (especially those that are small) are easy to make when they are rolled on a stick. Use various sized sticks (wooden skewers or dowel rods) to roll on. Roll tightly, to press out all the air.

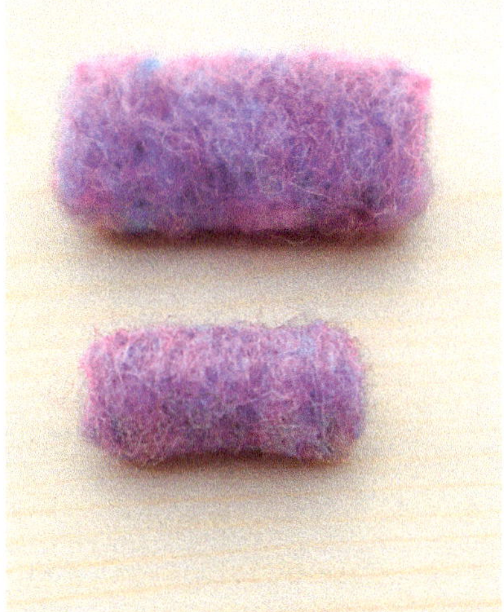

Slip the cylinder off the stick after rolling and felt around the middle and the sides.

Making a ball

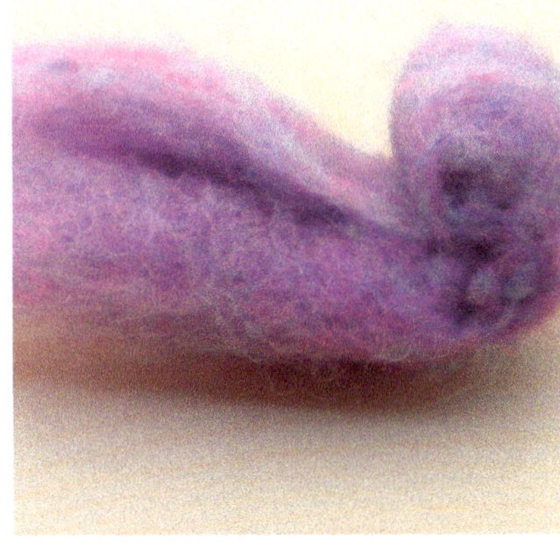

To make a ball, you can either roll a cyliner with a stick, or you can hand roll.
To hand roll, fold a piece of wool in half (and in half again for a smaller ball) and then begin rolling tightly. Felt with each turn of the roll.

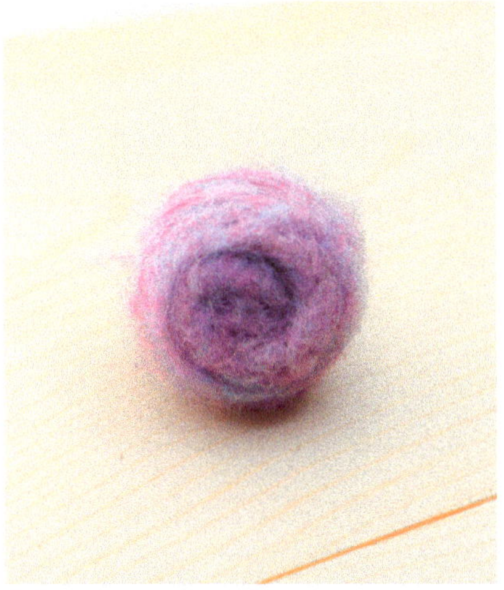

After it is completely rolled, tuck in the edges and felt firmly.

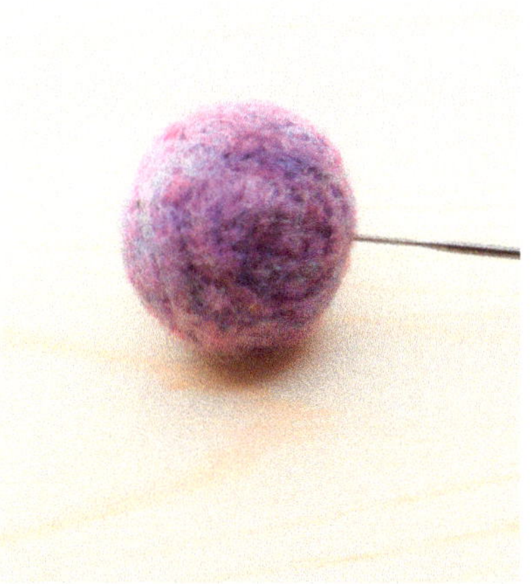

Turn the ball around as you continue to felt the entire area until you have a ball looking shape.

Rolling on a needle

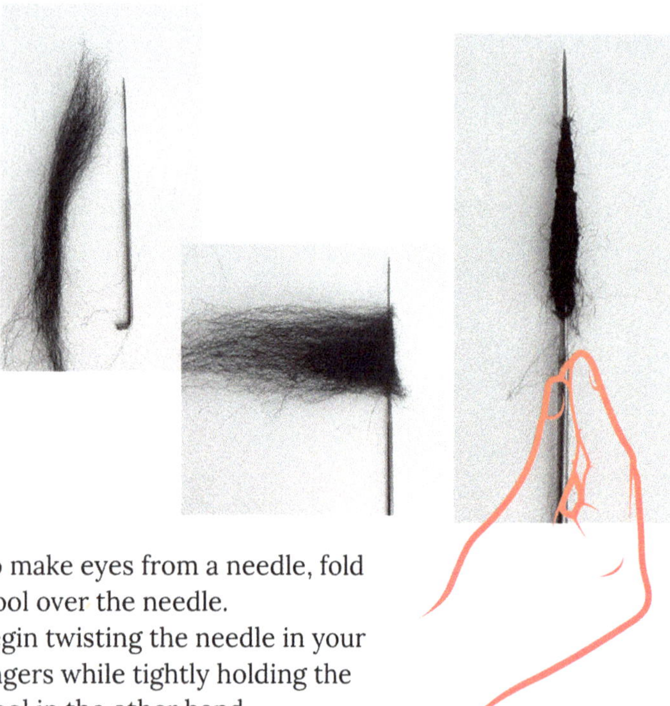

To make eyes from a needle, fold wool over the needle.
Begin twisting the needle in your fingers while tightly holding the wool in the other hand.

Rolled eyes

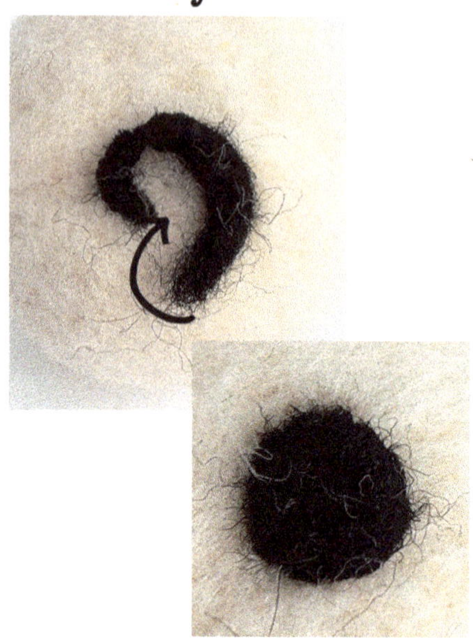

To make eyes from a needle roll, anchor the top of the roll in the eye area with a needle, then twist around into a circle, felting as you go. Finish the edges by going around the entire eye with your needle.

Shaping eyes

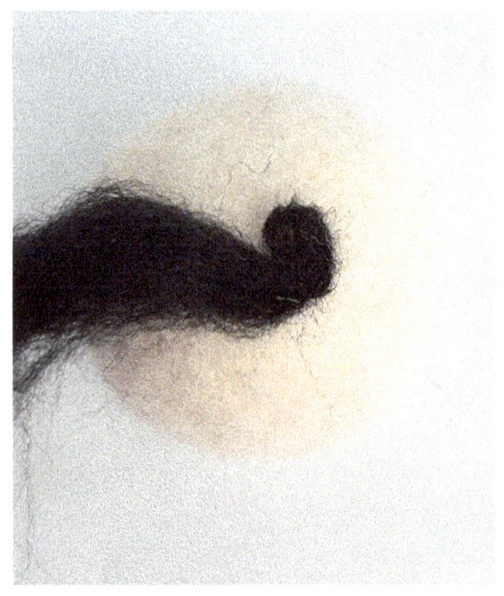

Another way to make a simple eye is by anchoring a piece of wool in the center, then wrapping the wool around that center, felting as you go.

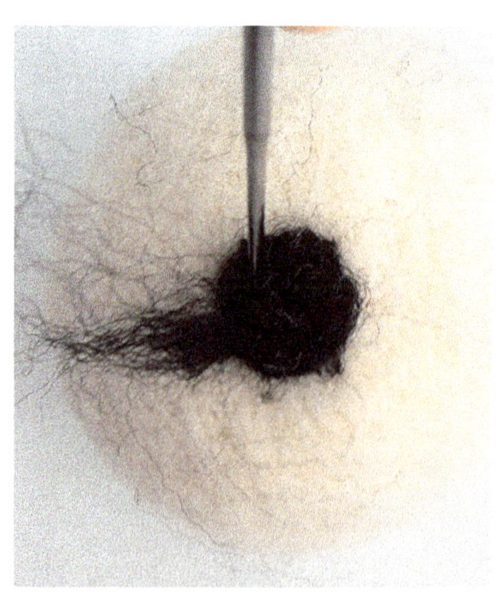

Continue to work around the edges, tucking in stray wool to neaten.

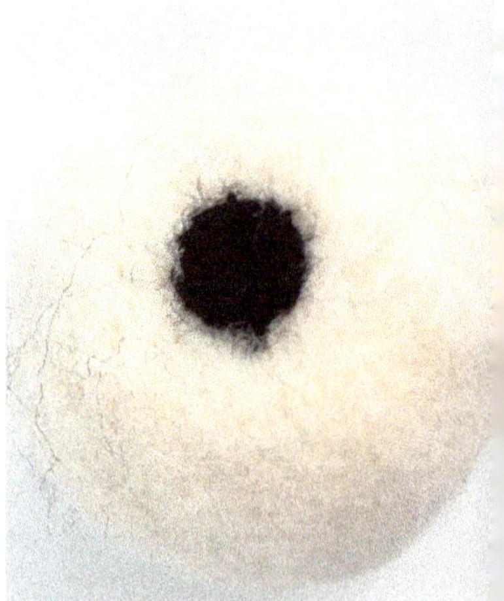

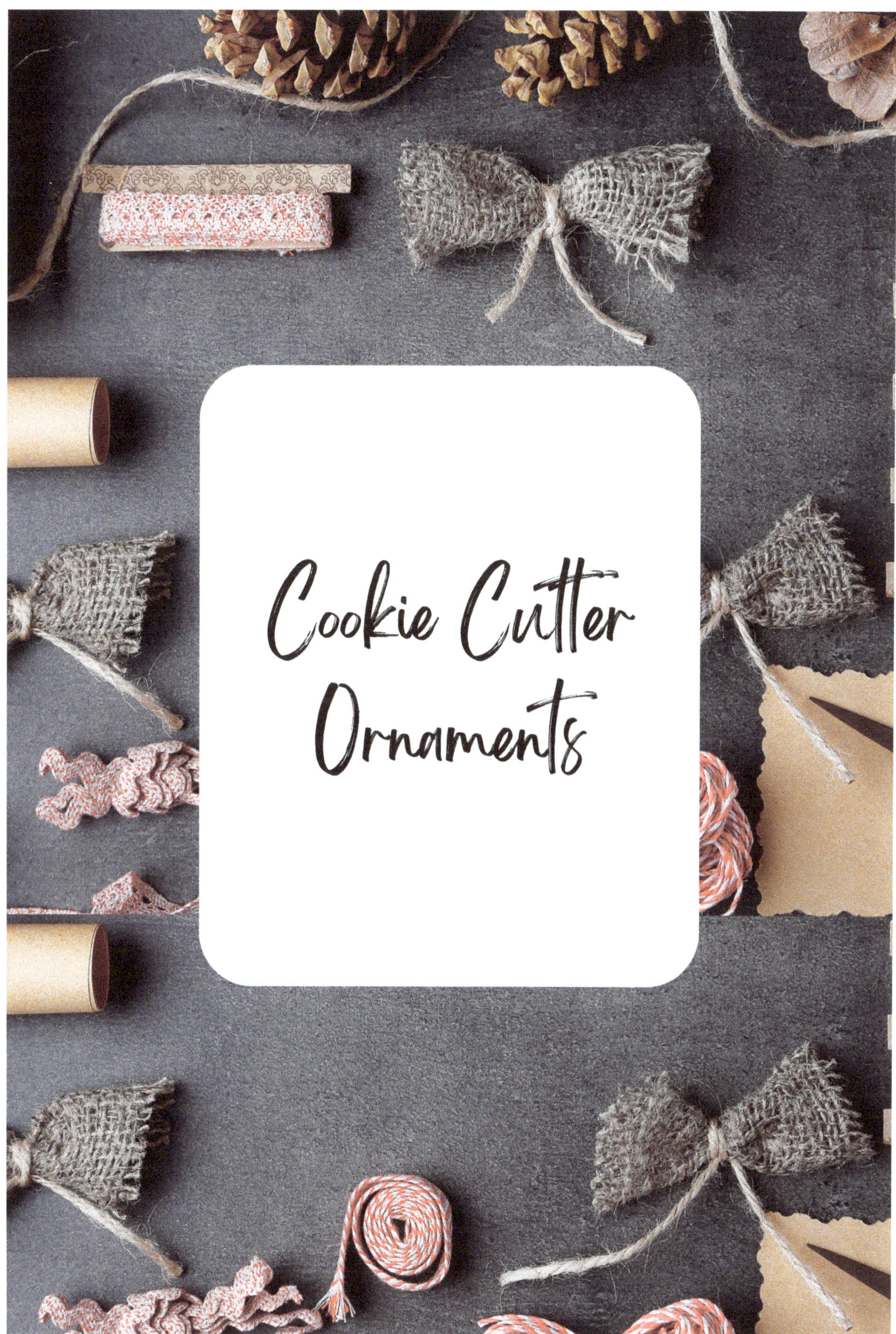

Cookie Cutter
Ornaments

Cookie Cutter Ornaments

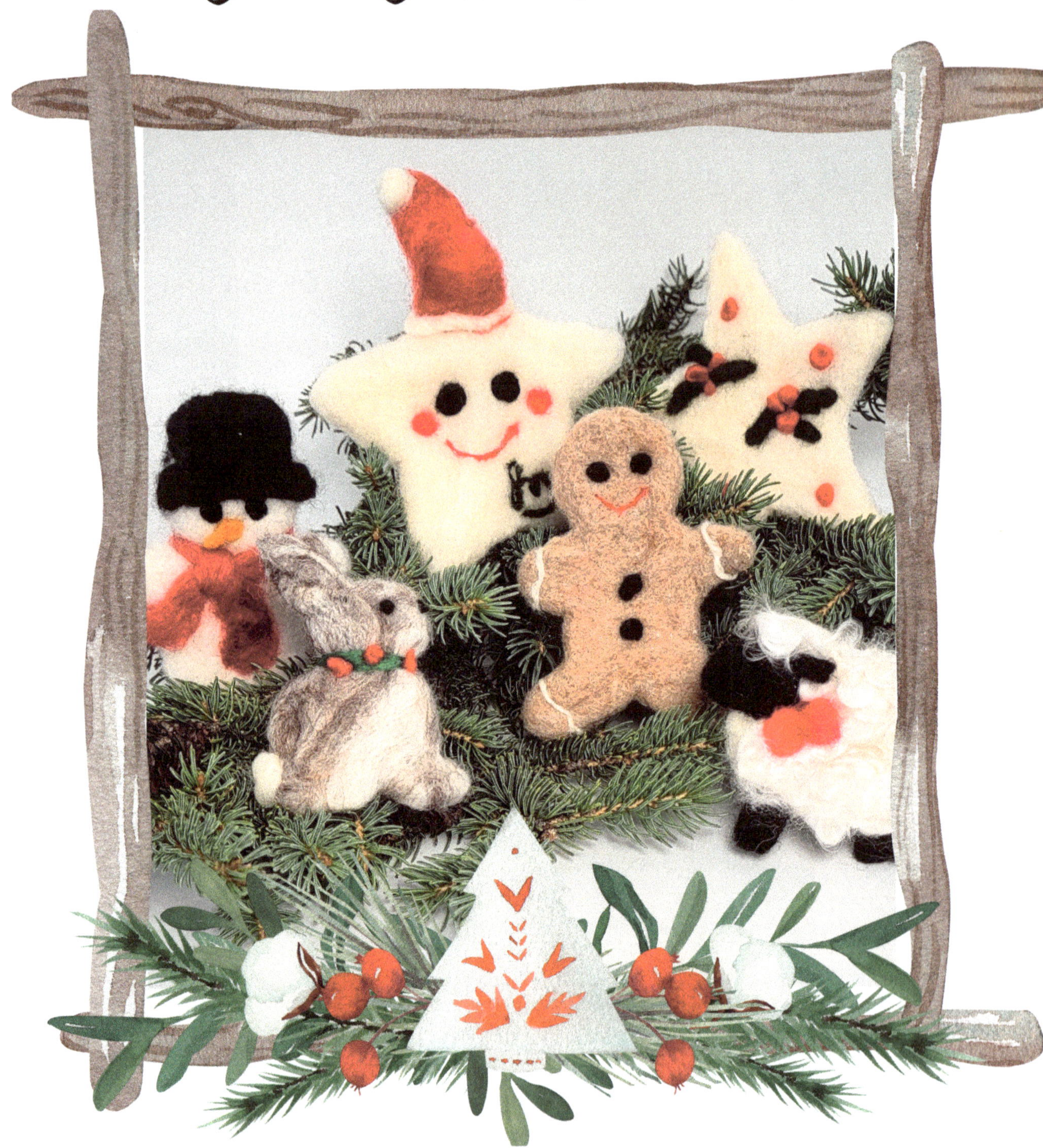

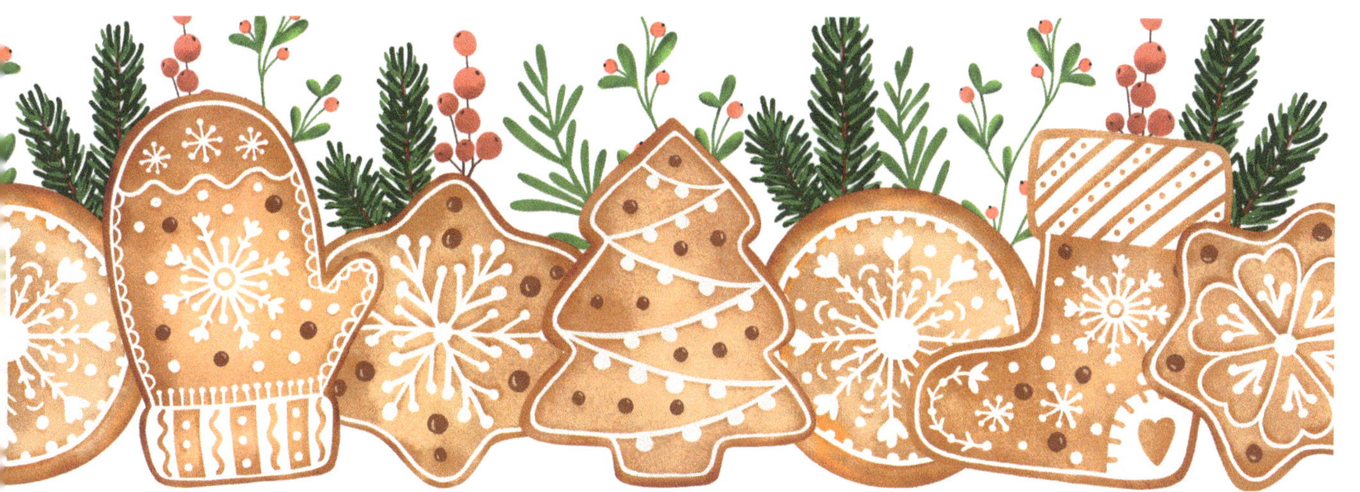

Cookie Cutter Tips

Cookie cutters are a great way for a beginner to get started as you don't have to worry about shaping the wool (because the margins are already defined for you) and it's great practice for learning how to felt firmly.

Not all cookie cutters are created equally when it comes to using them for felting. The cutters you use must not have a lip on the edge. Edges that have a small, overhanging lip will catch the needle and break it.

Make sure your cutters have clean edges (most metal cutters have clean edges).

Also, take great care and try not to hit the cutter with the needle as this will break the needle.

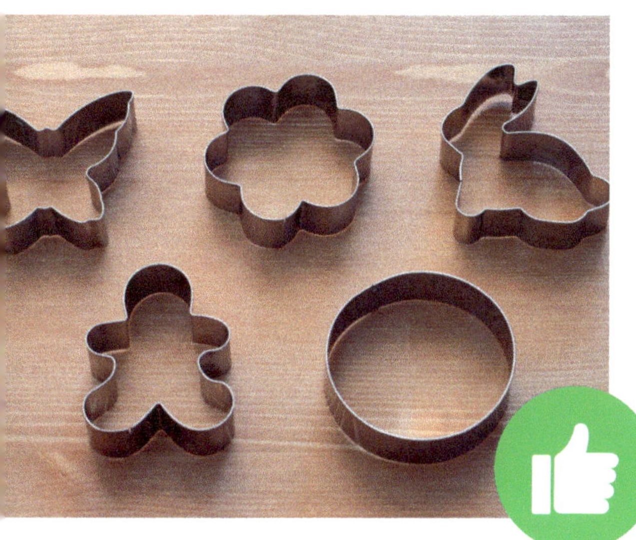

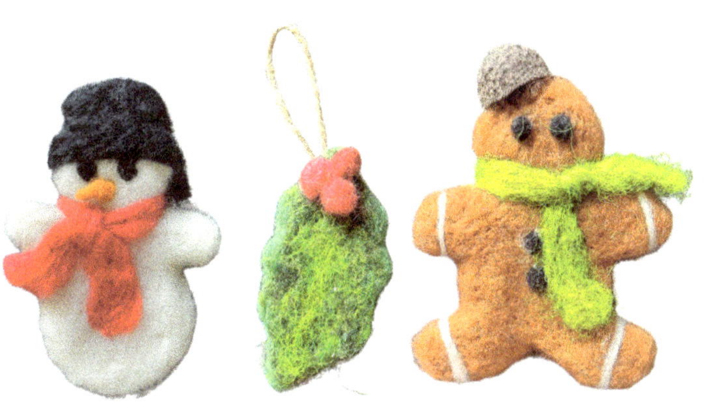

Gingerbread Man

- cookie cutter
- Batt-Brown/tan .25oz
- Small amounts batt: white, black, green or red

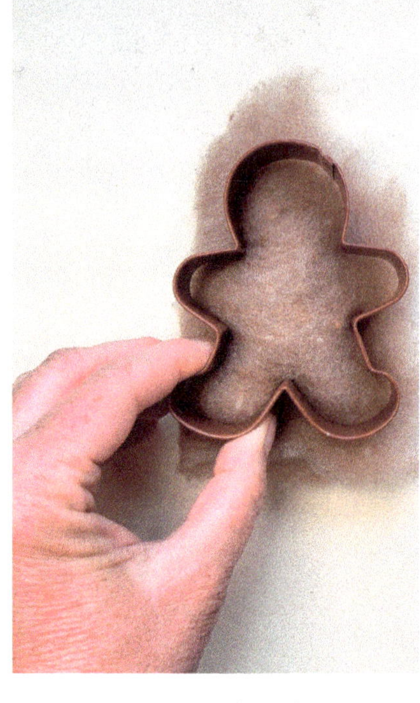

Measure a piece of tan batt to double the size of your cutter. Fold the batt in half.

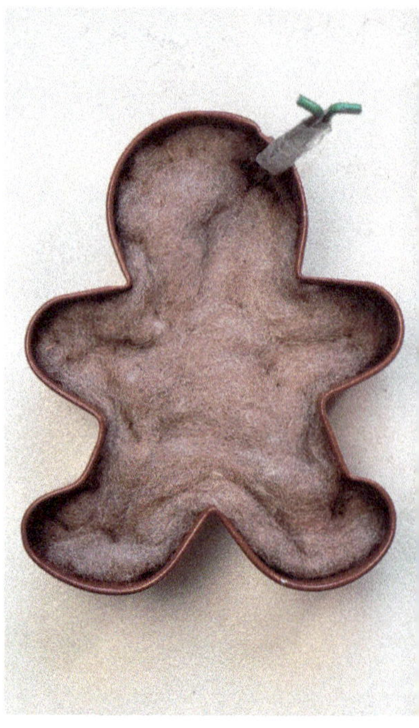

Push the batt into the cutter an begin by going around the outside of the cutter with your needle, being careful not to hit the cutter with the needle. Felt the middle.

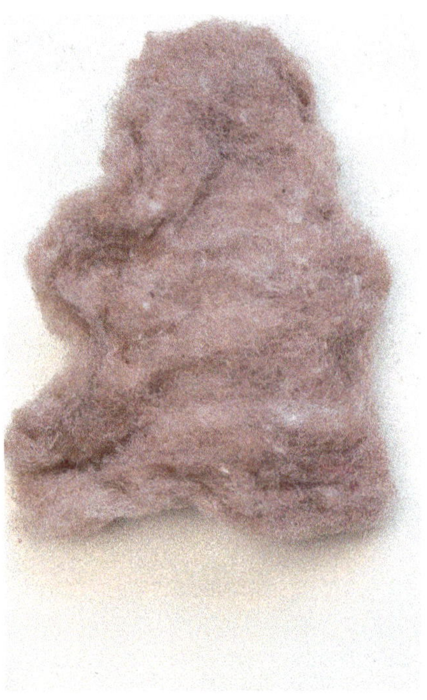

Take the piece out of the cutter, flip it over and push it back down into the cutter and felt the whole thing again. Repeat flipping and felting until your piece if firm and flat.

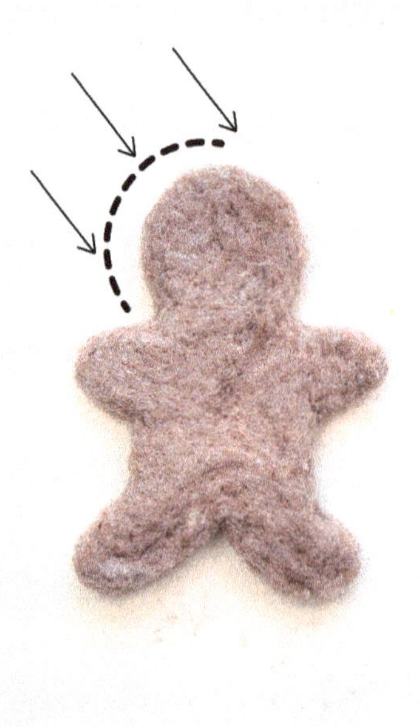

After your piece is the firm, take it out and use your needle to go around the edges to provide more definition.

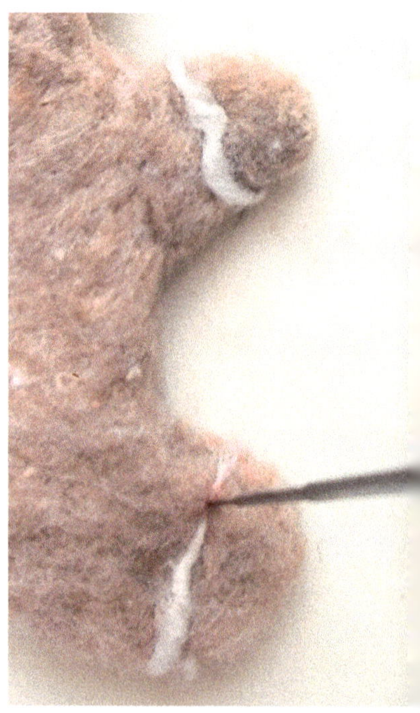

Add the "icing" to his limbs with white. Use thin strands of batt o top. Twist and felt down in a slight scallop pattern.

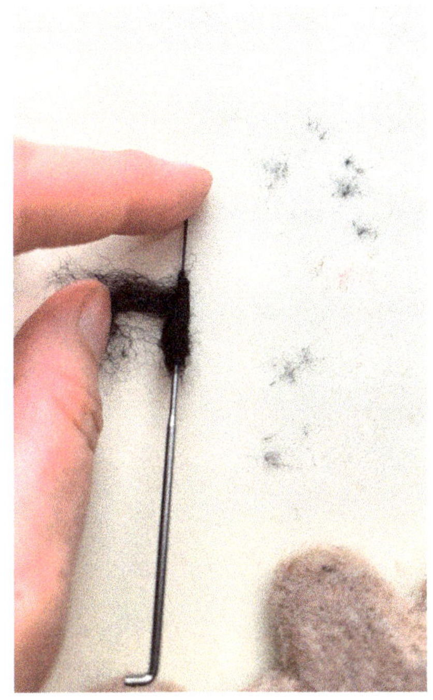

To make buttons and eyes, roll a small amount of black tightly around a needle.

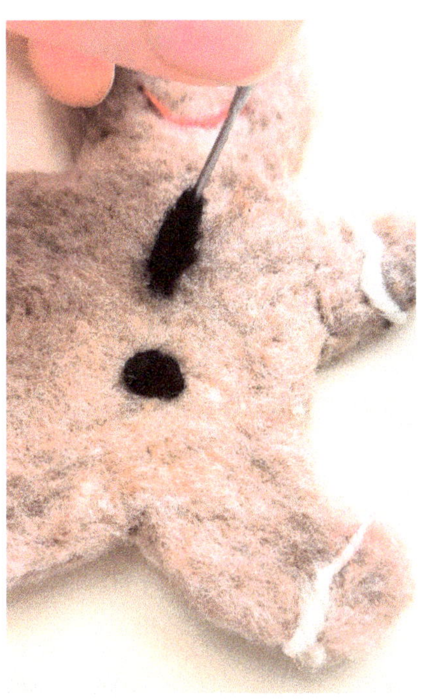

Push the needle into the wool and push off the rolled wool. Carefully felt this directly to the piece and neaten the edges by felting around the circle.

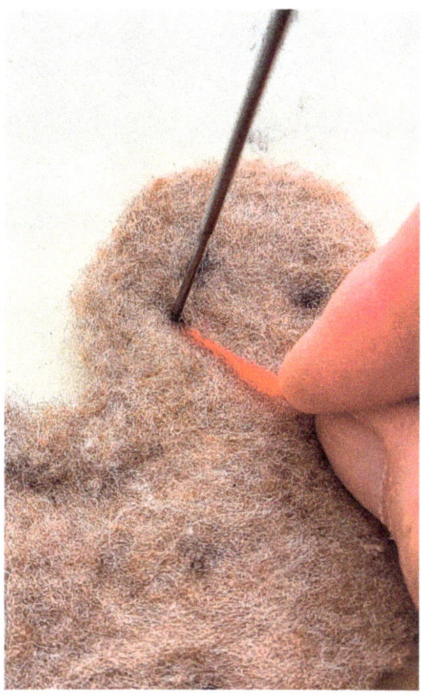

Using a thin red strand, anchor to one side of his mouth. Use another needle to felt while you shape the curve with your fingers.

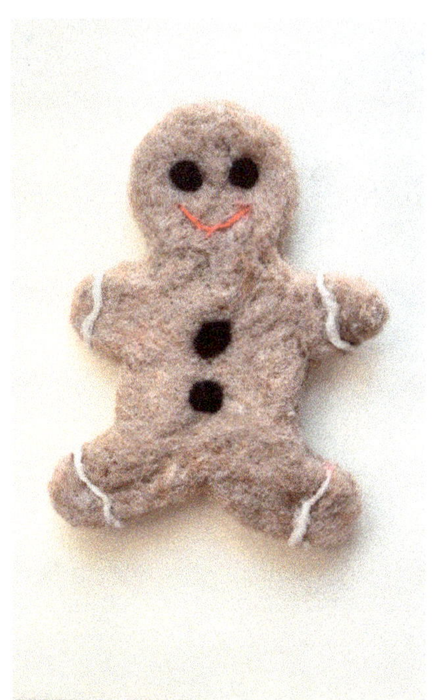

His main body is done! You can use him like this or decorate him with a scarf or bow tie, hat, etc...

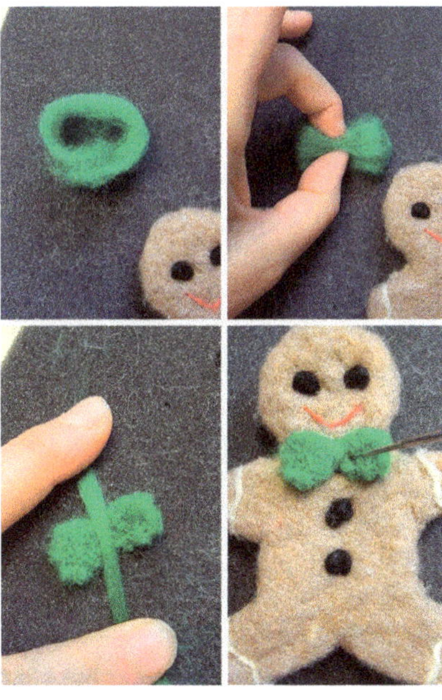

For a bow tie, wrap a small piece of wool around your finger and slip off. Pinch in the middle, then felt. Next, use a strand to tie around the middle and pull tight. Felt to his neck.

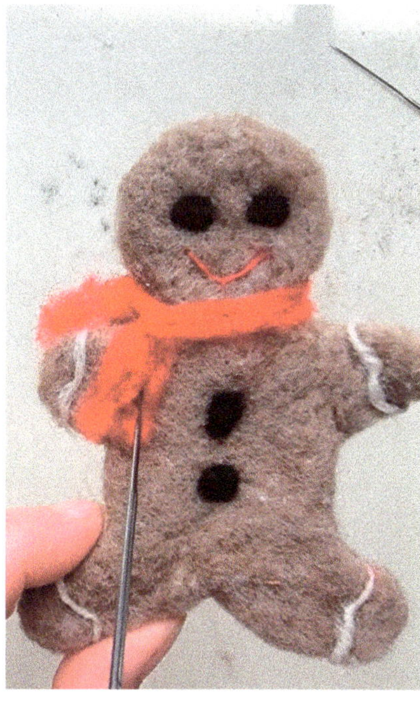

To make a scarf, tie wool around his neck and then felt directly to the piece.

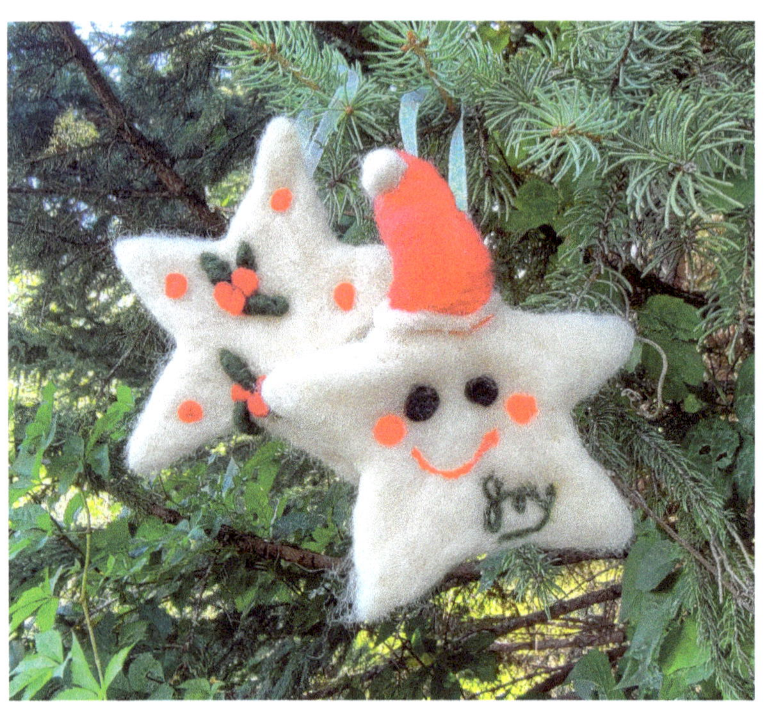

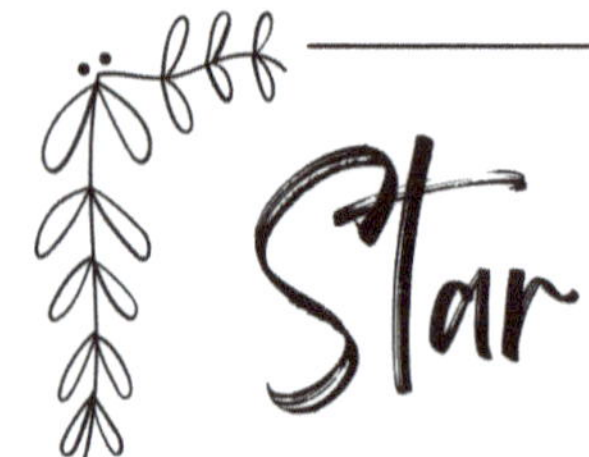

Star

- star cookie cutter
- Batt-natural/white (also called core wool) .25oz
- Small amounts batt: white, black, green or red

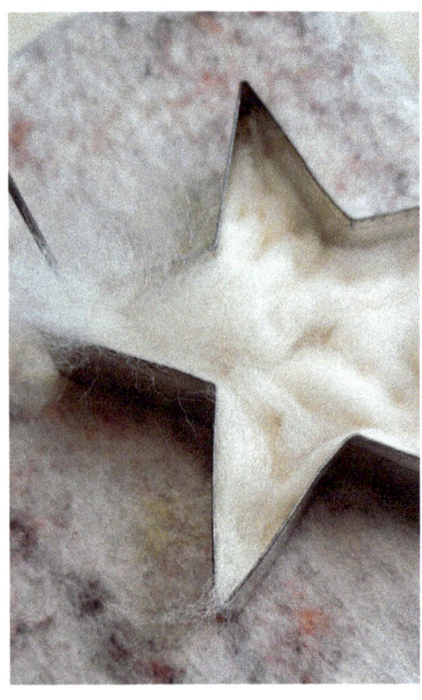

Felt the star-shaped cookie cutter (see Gingerbread man for more detailed base-shape directions).

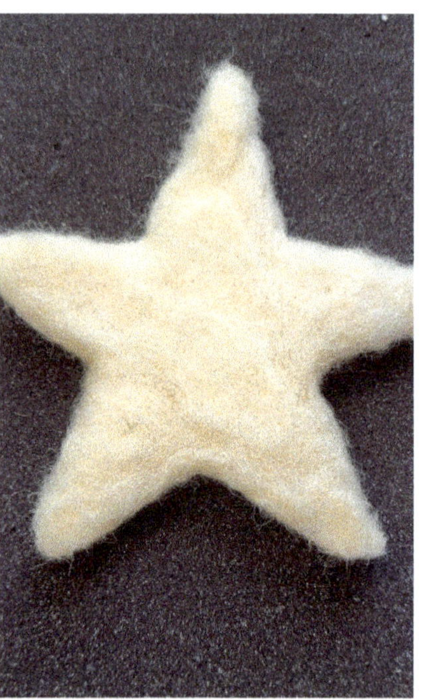

Go around the edges to neaten and also check for symetrical points.

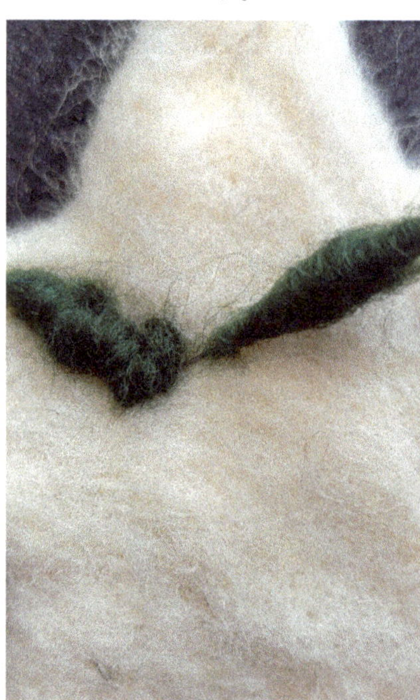

To make pieces of holly, wrap green wool tightly around the needle, slide off and felt directly to the star. Stab the holly with the needle to indent areas for a leaf shape.

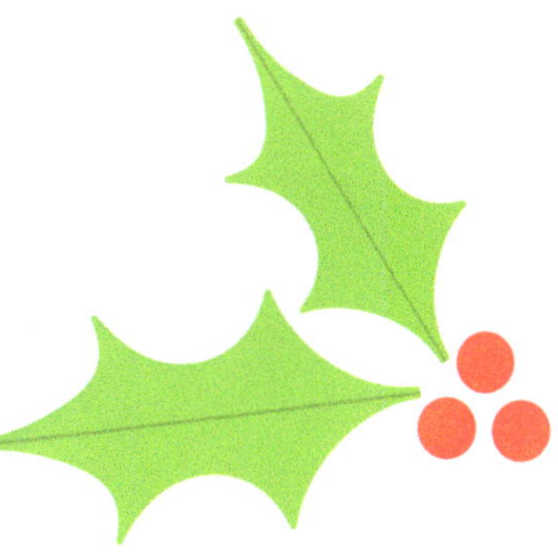

To make the berries, wrap red wool around your needle and push the needle into the star where you want to place the berry. Felt directly onto the star to shape the berry.

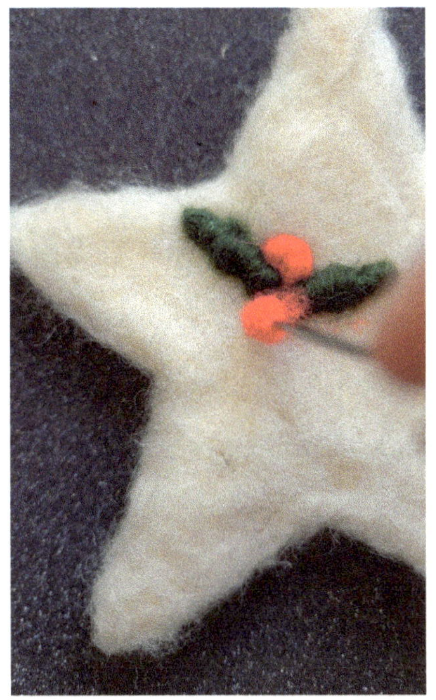

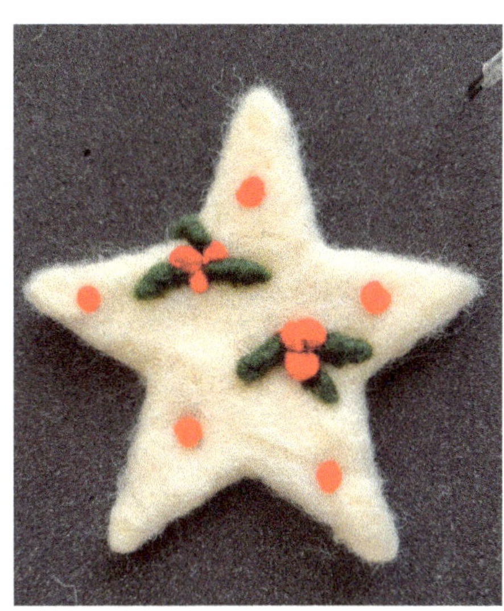

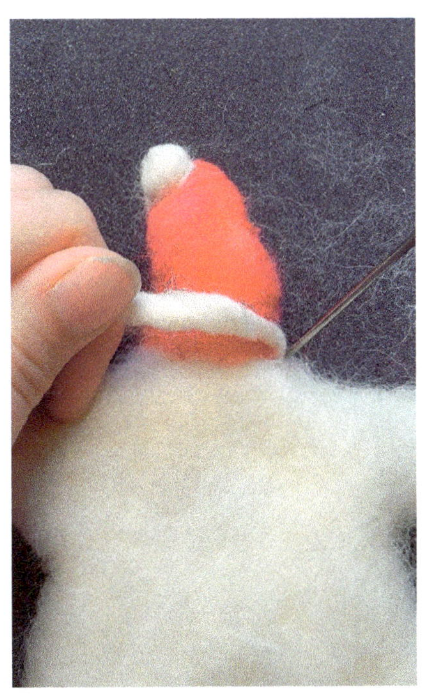

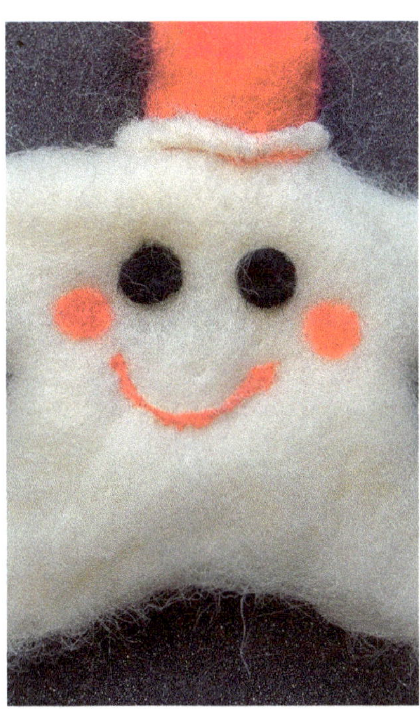

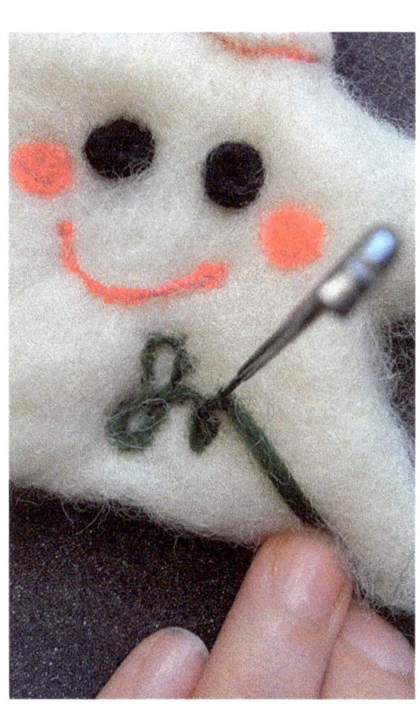

To make a Santa star, wrap the top point with red wool and felt down. Next, twist white wool and felt to the bottom of the hat. Finally, make a white pom for the top by wrapping the needle with white wool and sliding and felting directly to the top.

Make eyes and cheeks with the needle rolling technique and felt directly to the face.

For the mouth, use a thin strand of red, anchor on one end with a needle while you shape and felt with another needle.

You can needle felt short words in cursive. Twist a thin strand and anchor with a needle, while you twist into letters, felting down as you go.

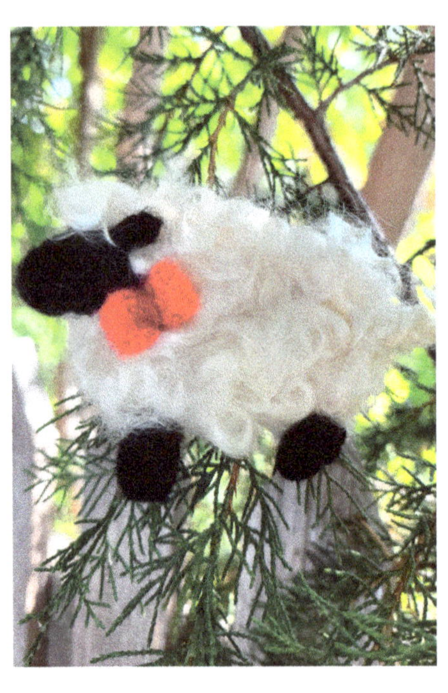

Sheep

- Sheep cutter

- Batt-natural/white

  (also called core wool)

  .25oz

- Optional: white locks*

- Small amounts batt:

  white, black, green, red

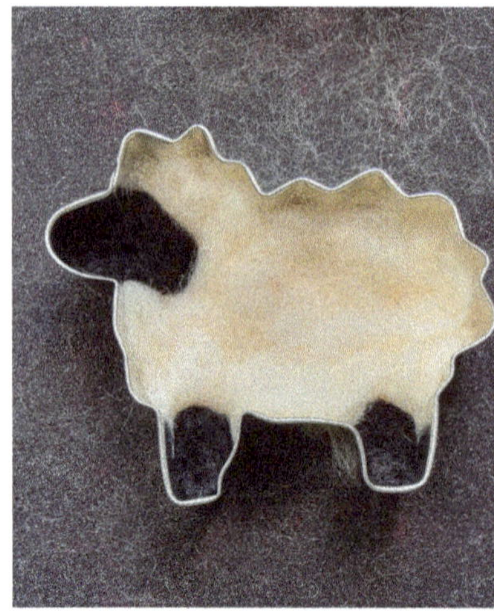

Place white wool in the middle o
the cutter and then add the blacl
wool as shown. Felt down firmly

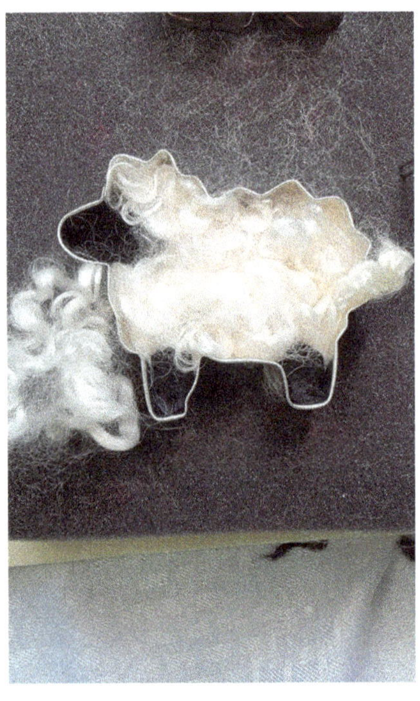

If you have them, add curly locks
to the top. Do not felt down
firmly, be gentle. This will help
the locks to retain their curl.

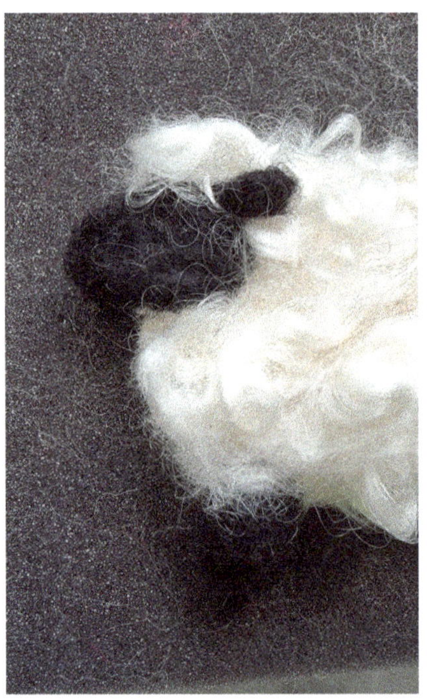

Twist some black wool into an
ear shape as shown, felt to the
top edge of the face.

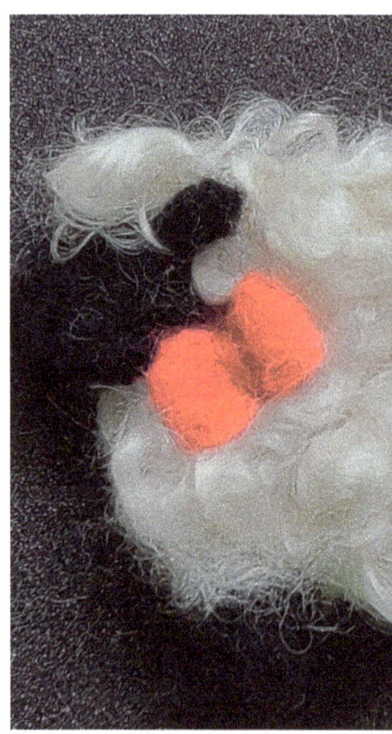

Add a bow or a scarf (directio
under gingerbread man proje

***White Locks are the curly, uncombed part of the sheeps or goats coat. It's a finishing
fiber that is very versatile for decorating the tops of your projects.**

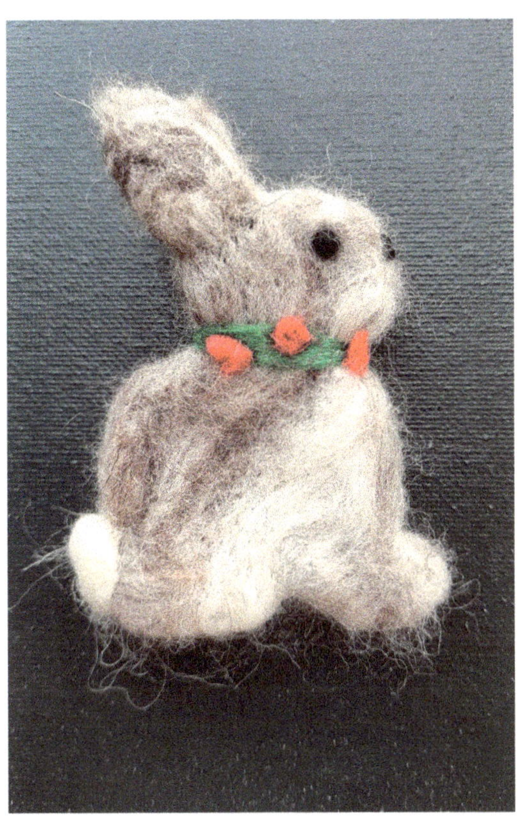

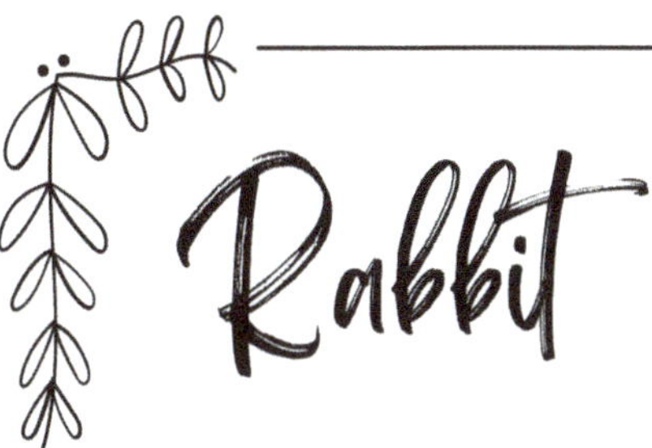

Rabbit

- Rabbit Cutter
- Batt-natural/white (also called core wool) .25oz
- Batt-tan .25oz
- Small amounts batt: white, black, green or red

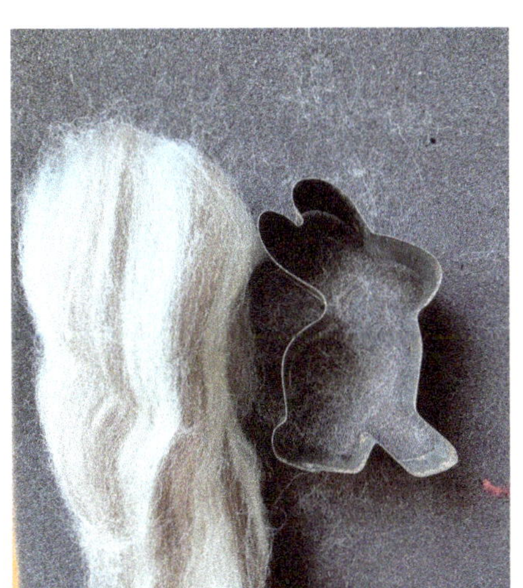

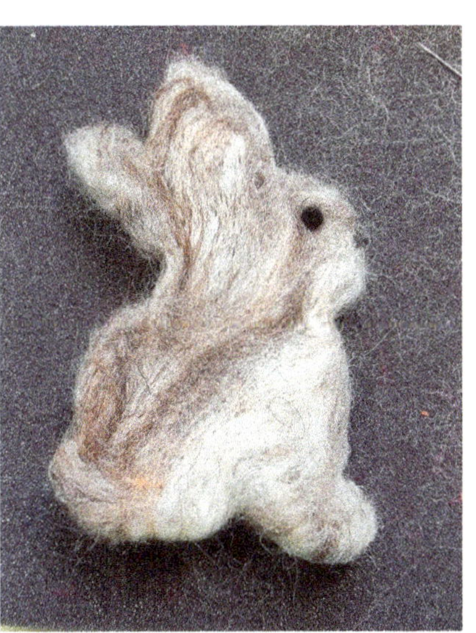

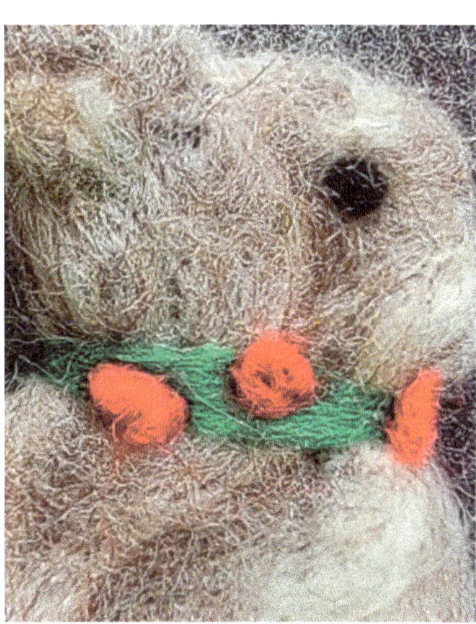

You can make a two-toned piece by using two colors of wool. You can either buy batt that is striated (as shown) or you can pull apart different colors and lay them next to each other before you place them in the cutter.

Felt the rabbit firmly then add a small eye and nose using the needle wrapping method. Add a tail with the needle wrapping method.

Add some green in a thin strand and felt down. Next, make berries as shown in the star project. You can also give him a scarf or even a hat.

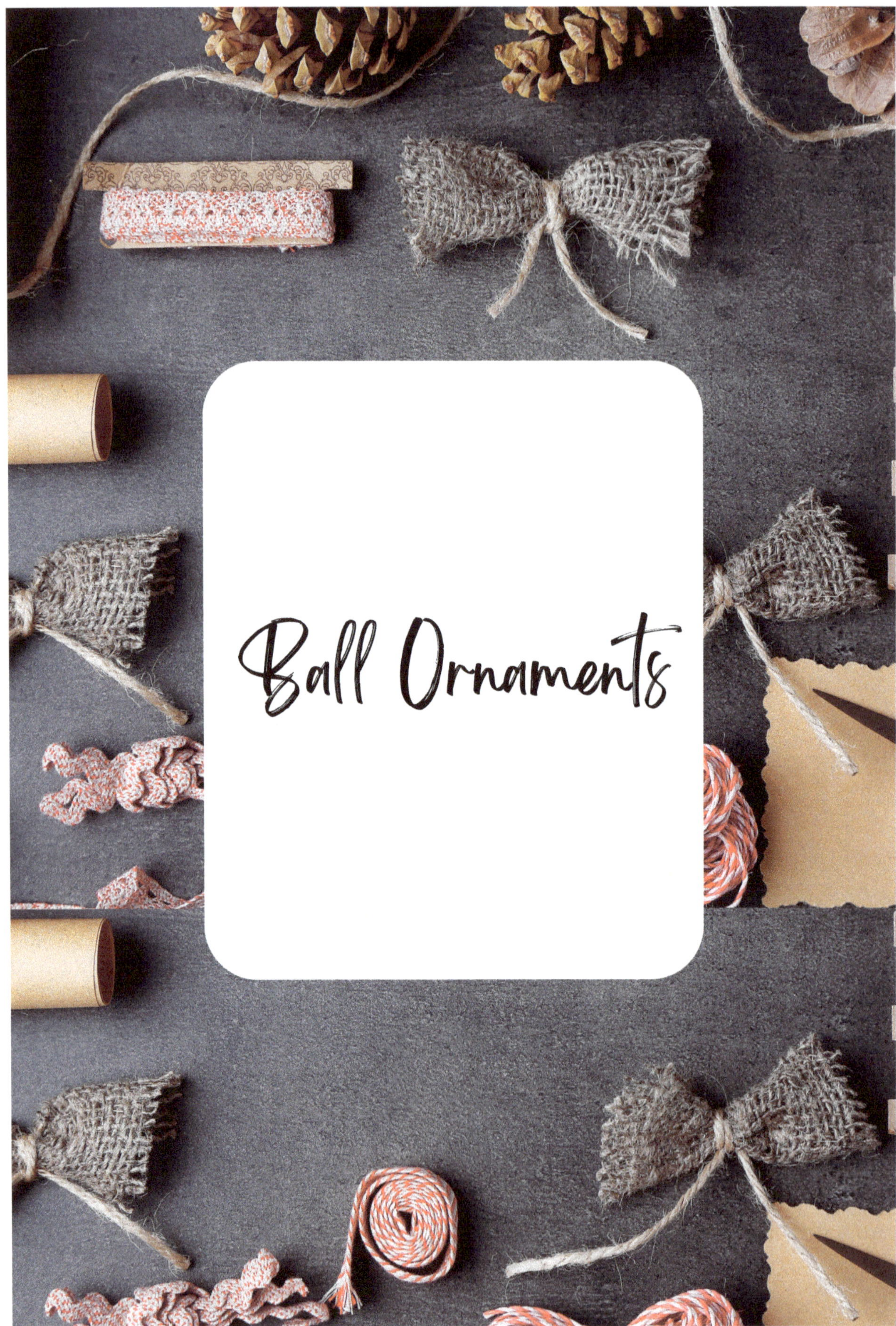

Ball Ornaments

Ball Ornaments

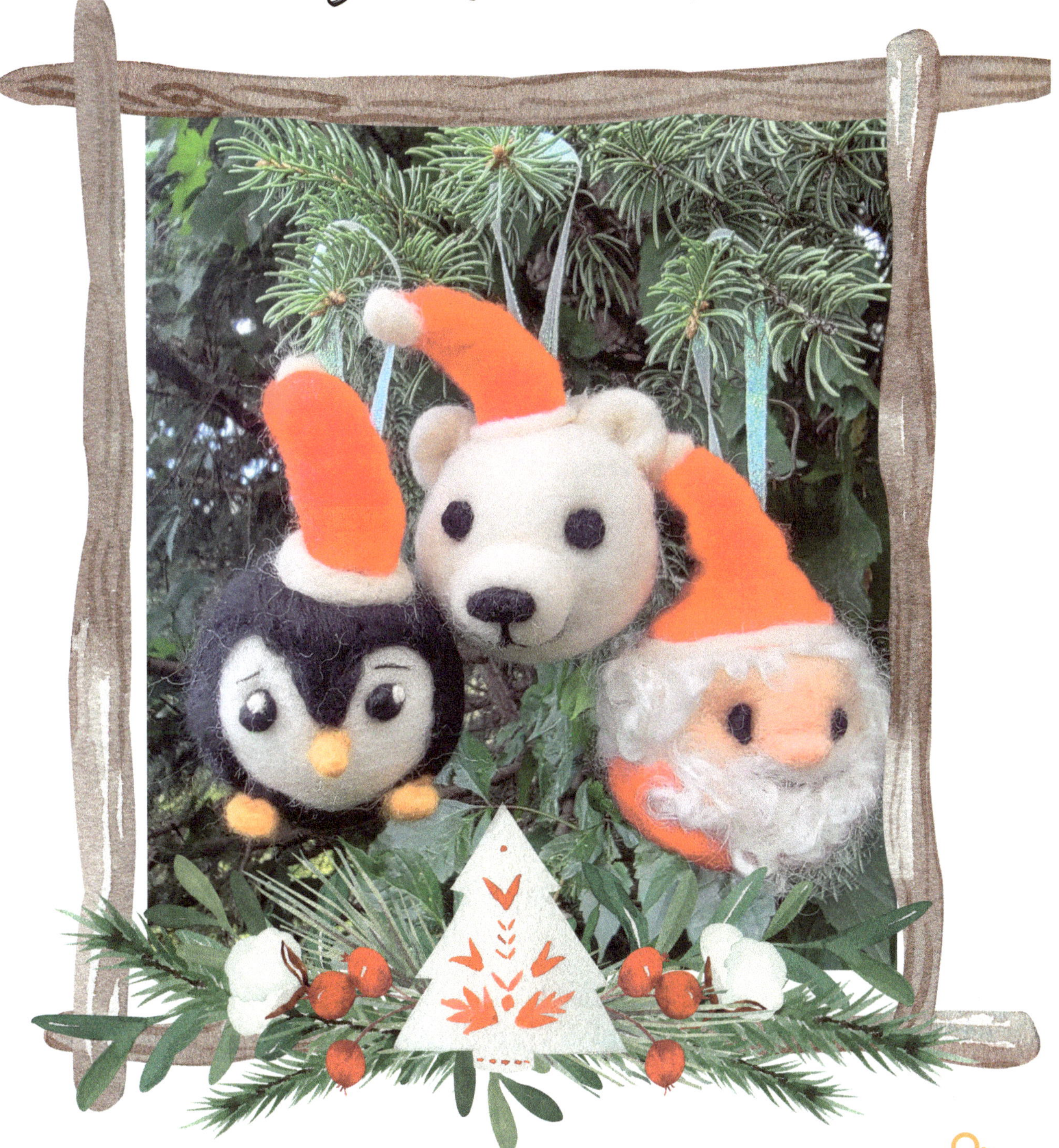

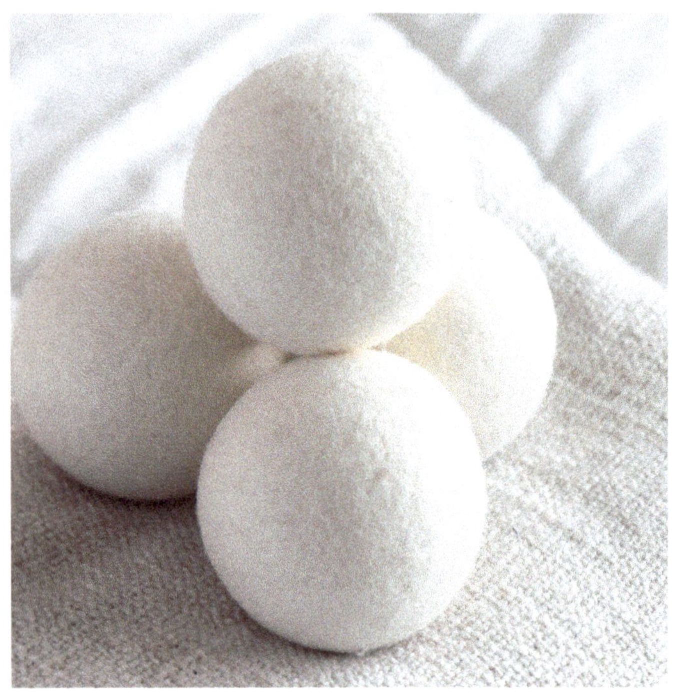

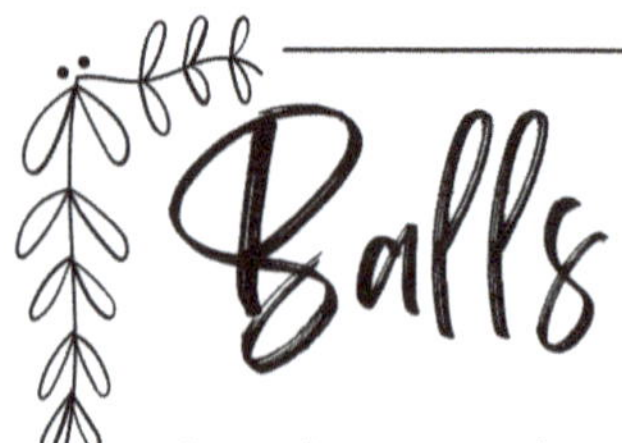

- Batt/core wool - .50 oz (14.17g)

- Optional: tights or pantyhose

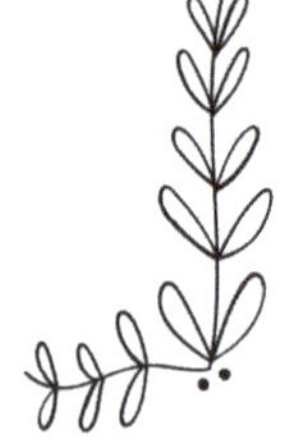

Method 1: stick roll

Method 2: hand roll

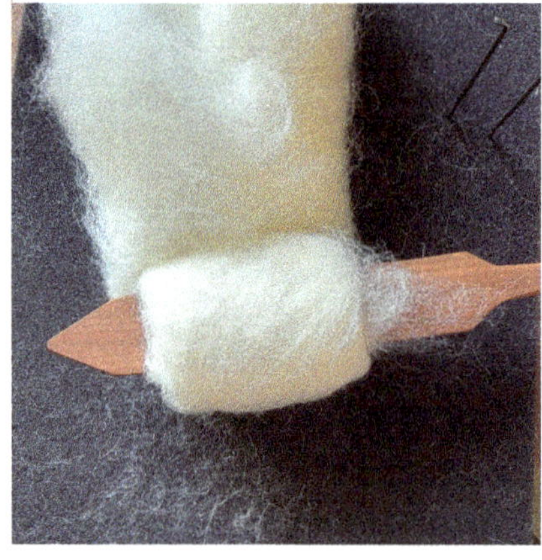

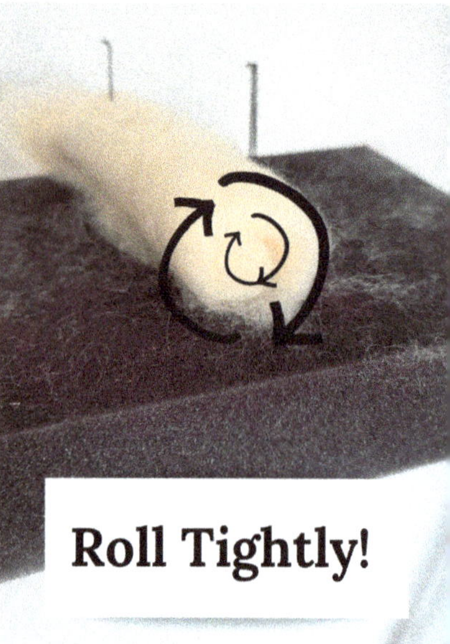

Roll Tightly!

Weigh out the core/natural batt wool. .5 oz or 14.17 g.
I like weighing the wool as opposed to measuring because batts come in different thickness, you will get a more uniform product if you weigh it out.

To create a well-formed, compact ball, my preferred technique involves folding the batt into thirds and then rolling it onto a wooden stick. This minimizes the amount of felting required. After rolling, gently remove it from the stick and proceed with the felting process.

At this point, you can choose to continue felting to shape it into a ball or opt for the pantyhose wash and dry method.

Fold the batt into thirds until it becomes the width that you desire and then roll it tightly.

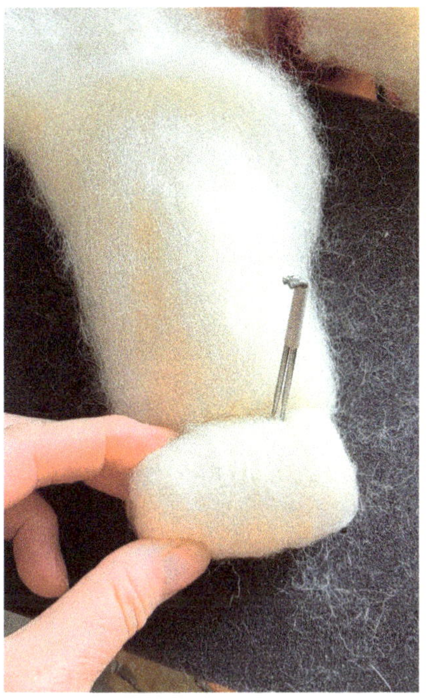

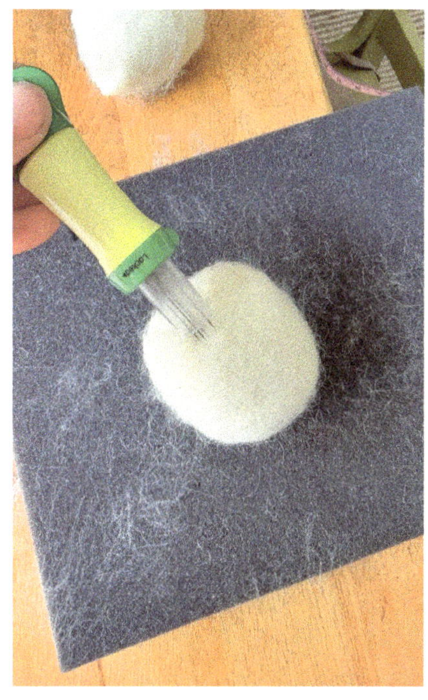

Optional: Time saving pantyhose method

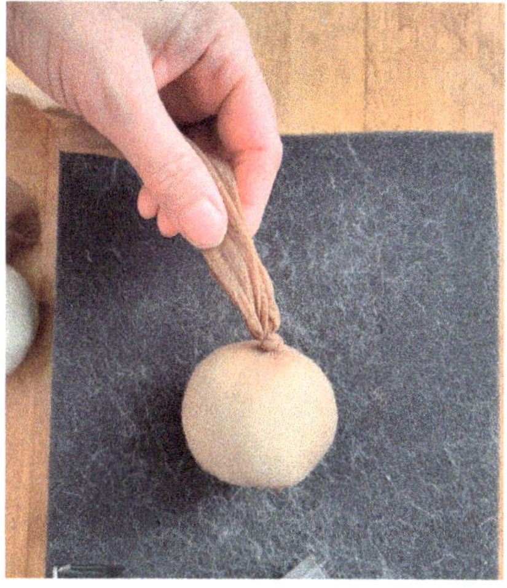

Begin rolling from the bottom and felt with each turn.

Continue to turn the ball over and over, felting as you go. A multi needle tool is very helpful for this type of work.

If you want to save time, skip the final step of felting and use the panty hose/washer method instead. It's fast and saves stabbing time.

Simply take a loose ball (done with either method above) and stuff it into a leg of hoisery. Tie the hoisery tightly at the top with a knot. You can usually fit up to 5 balls per leg.

Use this method to make dryer balls too!

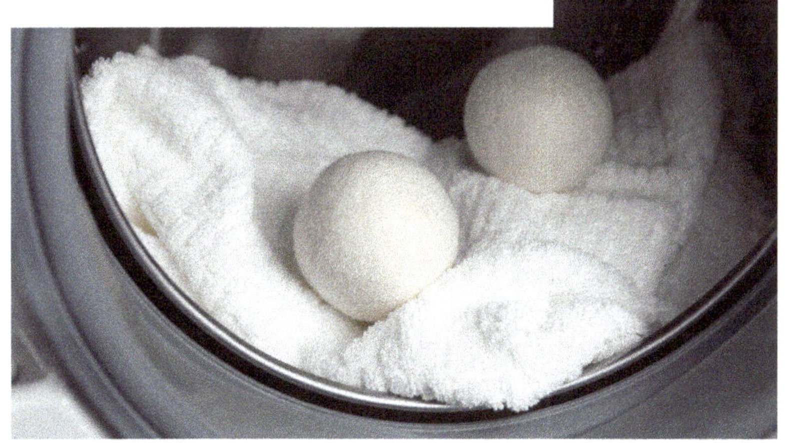

Before and After Washing and drying

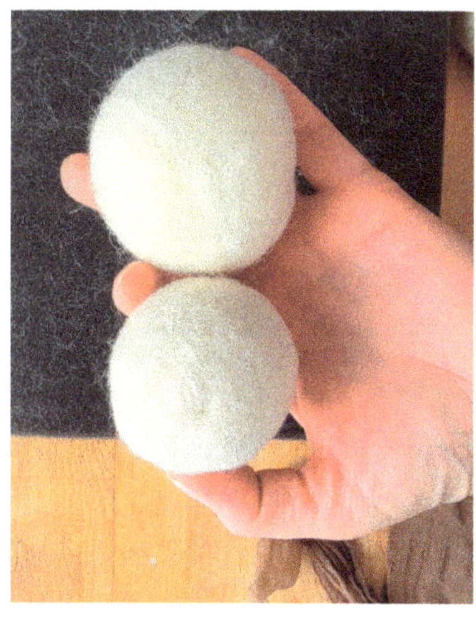

Next, put it into the washer with like colors, I use the hot setting. After it's done washing, put it into the dryer with the other clothes on a high setting. The machines will felt them for you! You may need to neaten up the balls a bit after you remove them from the pantyhose, but the machines have done most of the work!

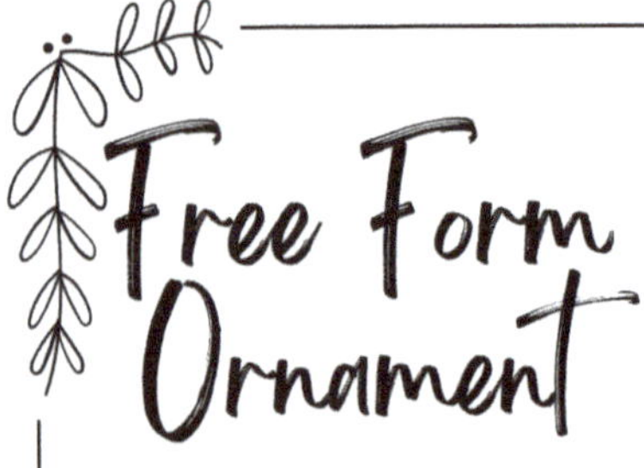

Free Form Ornament

- . 5 oz Wool Ball

- Small amounts:
  green, red or any
  color you choose

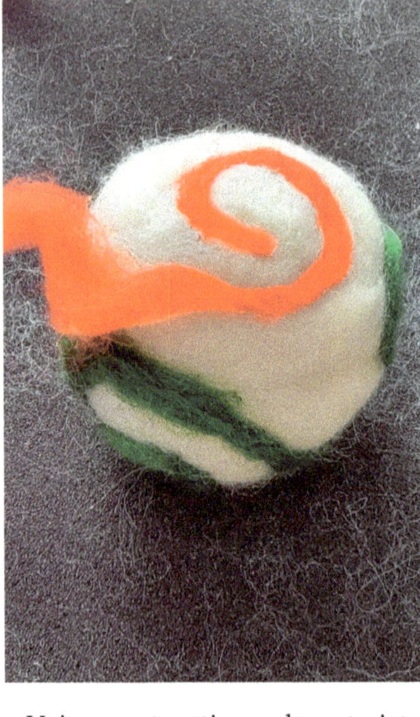

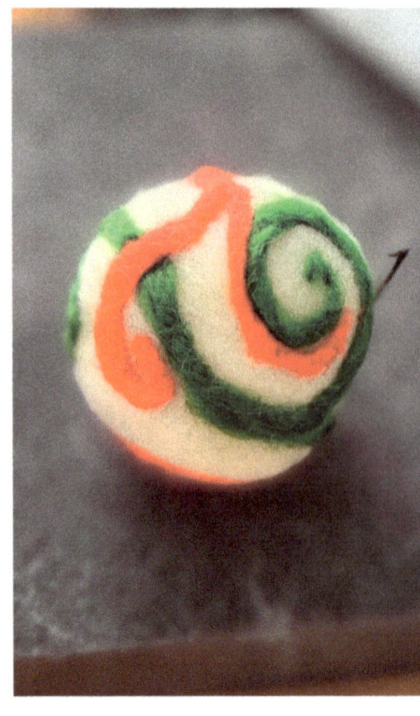

Using contrasting colors, twist
strands of wool and anchor
them to the ball with a needle.

With another needle, felt down
the strands in a random,
twirling pattern.

Bear

- .5 oz wool ball
- Wool/natural or
  white, matching wool
- Small amounts: Black,
  red
- small round dowel

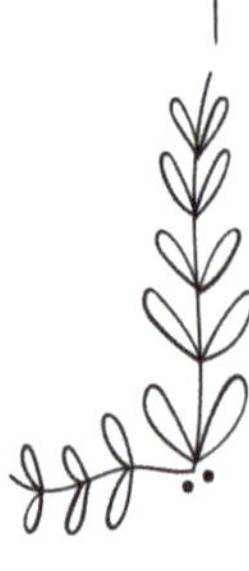

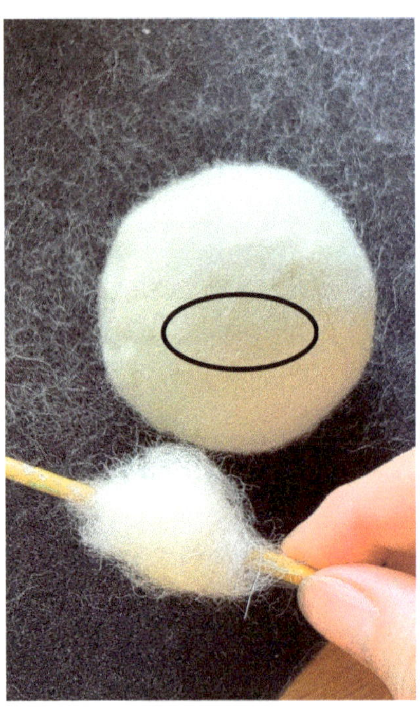

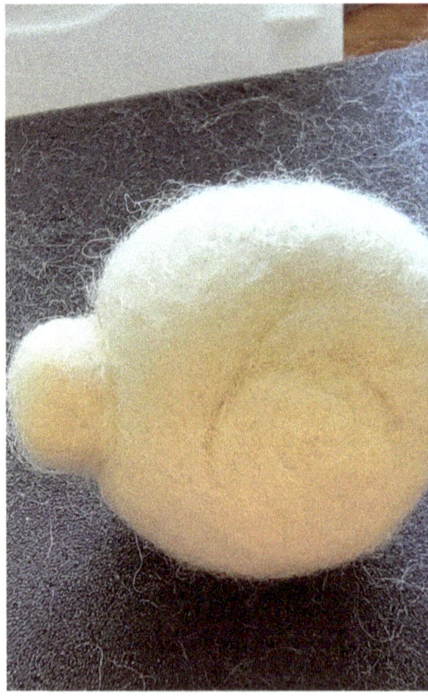

Start by making the bears
muzzle. Wrap a piece of wool
around a thin stick, you are
aiming for an oval shape.

Slide the muzzle carefully off the
stick, place onto the face and felt
securely.

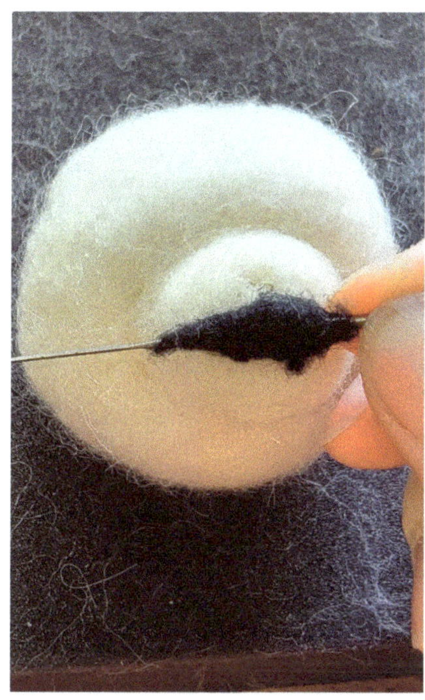

Make the nose as you did the muzzle but use a needle. Slide black nose off the needle, place onto the middle of the muzzle and felt.

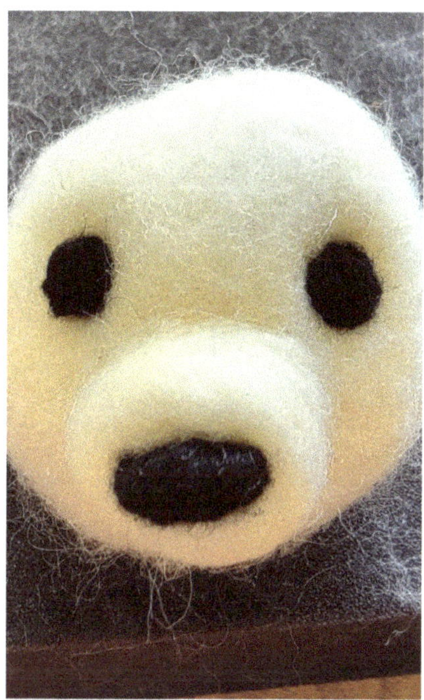

For eyes, wrap black around a needle, place into eye socket and twist the roll into a circular shape. Felt down. See "Basic Techniques" for making eyes from needle rolled wool.

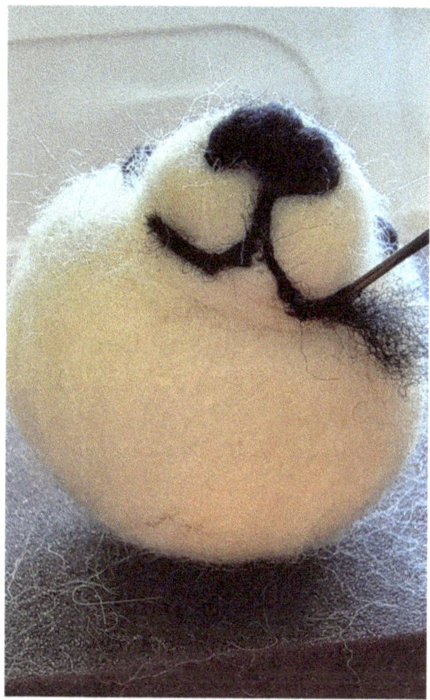

Using thin strands, make the mouth as shown and felt down. Take care when felting thin strands as it is easy to push them too far into the wool and "lose" them. Use an easy touch.

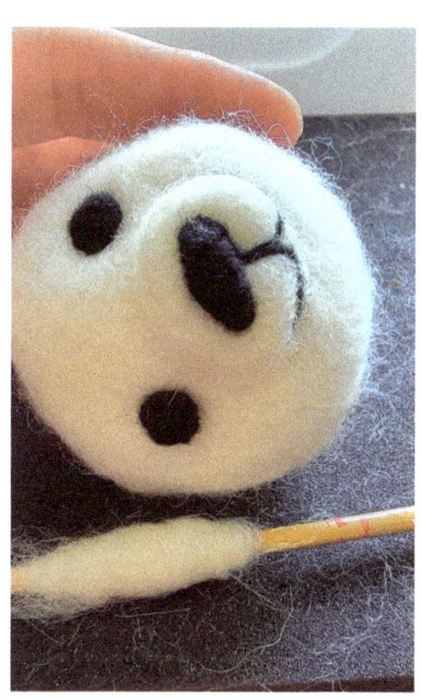

For the ears, roll wool onto a thin stick.

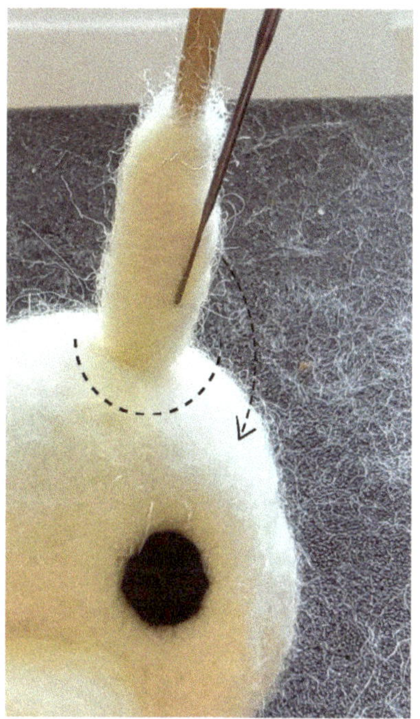

Poke the stick onto the ear area of the head. While the wool is still on the stick, felt around the bottom of the ear to attach it.

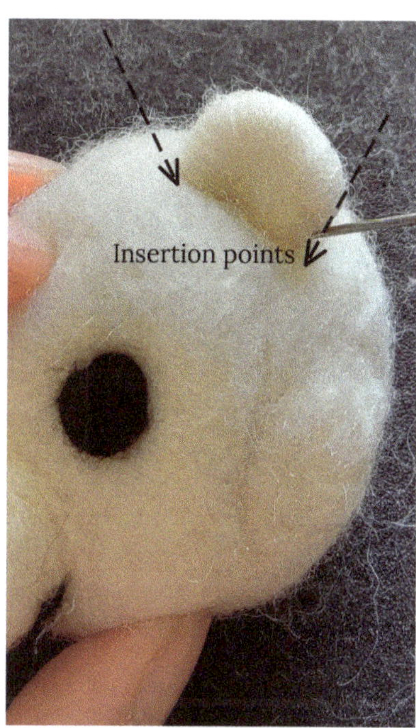

Slide the wool off the stick and bend the wool piece over to the other side of the ear attachment area and felt down.

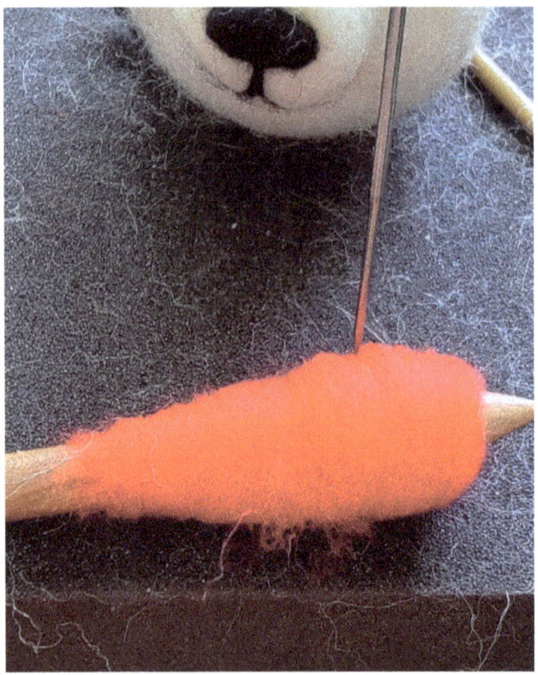

To make the hat, roll red wool on a stick,
make the bottom end thicker than the top.
Felt carefully around the stick to firm it up
before you take it off the stick. Roll off stick.

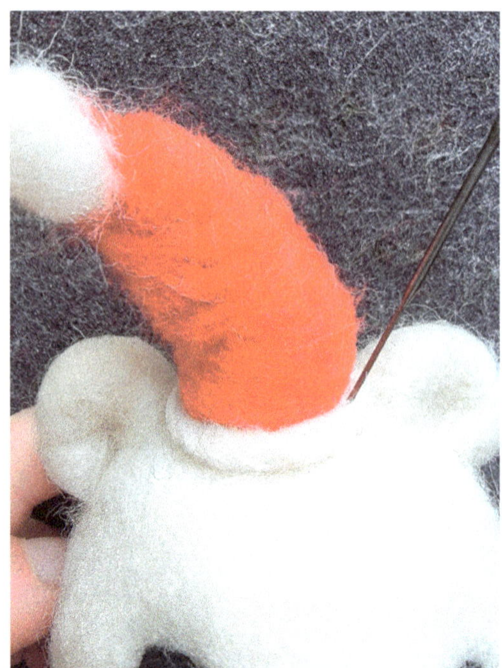

Attach to the head by felting around the
bottom edge.
Next, twist some white wool and felt
around the bottom of the hat. Make a
pom for the top of the hat and felt on.

Everyone loves this polar bear! He is
one of my most requested ornaments!

If you are interested in selling them,
they make a good profit as they only
take about 20 minutes to create the
face.

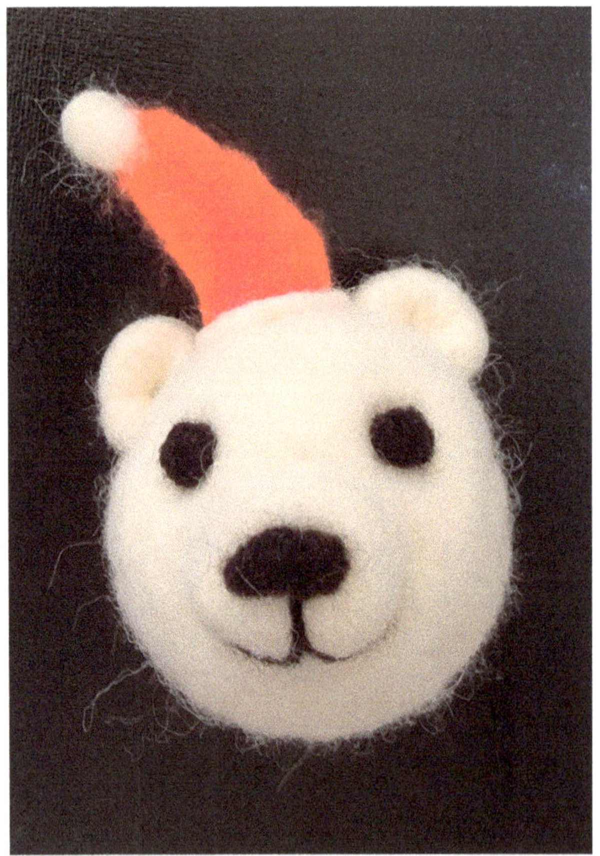

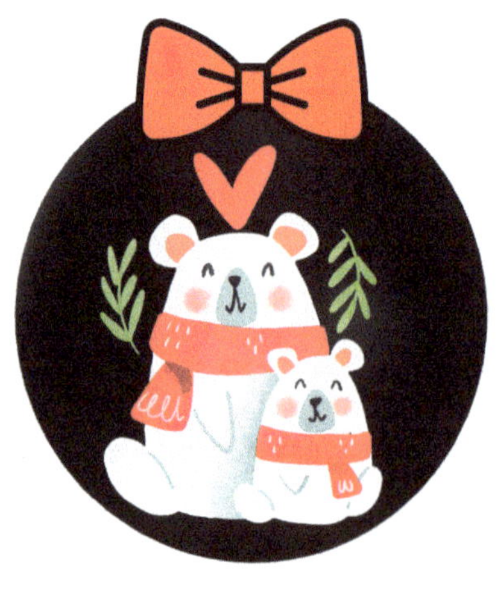

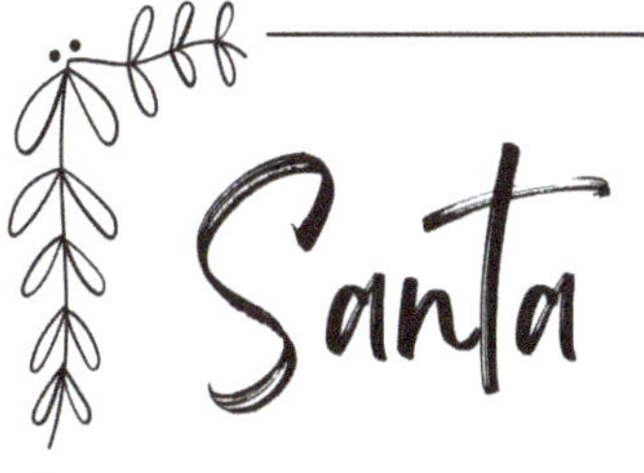

Santa

- .5 oz Wool ball
- Wool/natural or white
- Curly locks
- Small amounts: Black, red, peach
- small round dowel

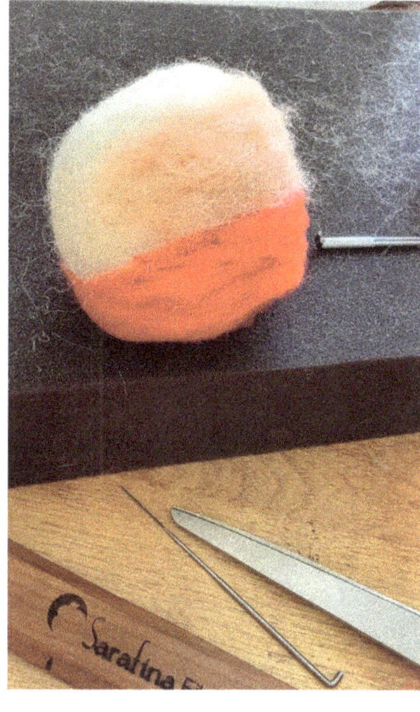

Cover a ball with red on the bottom, peach or flesh color for the face.

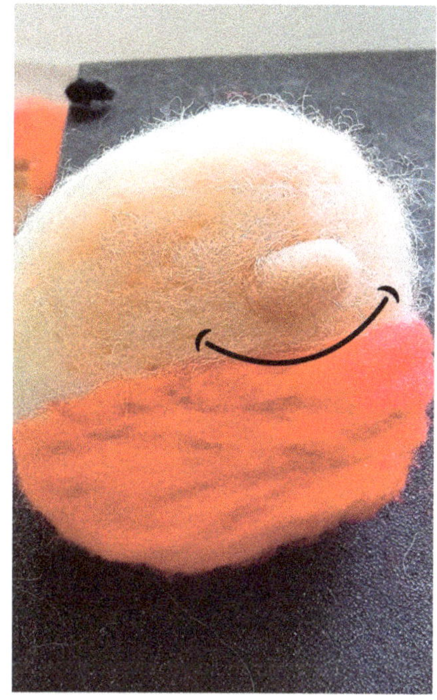

Make a nose by rolling on a needle, slide off and attach to the face. Add a smile with thin, black wool.

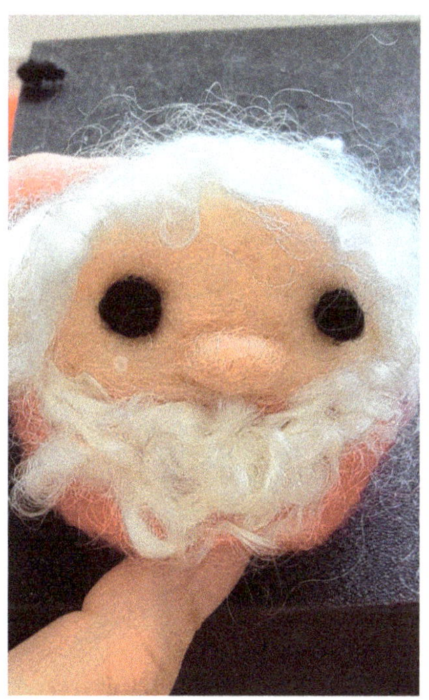

Create eyes (as shown in the polar bear).
Make a beard and add hair out of curly locks or white batt. Use a gentle hand when attaching so the curls or batt don't lose their fluffy appearance.

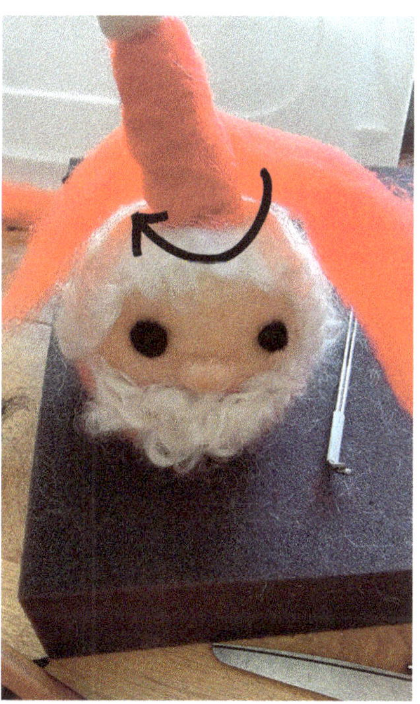

Make a hat as with the polar bear above, by rolling on a stick. To make the hat larger, add wool to the bottom of the base of the hat and felt down. Use white wool to trim the hat.

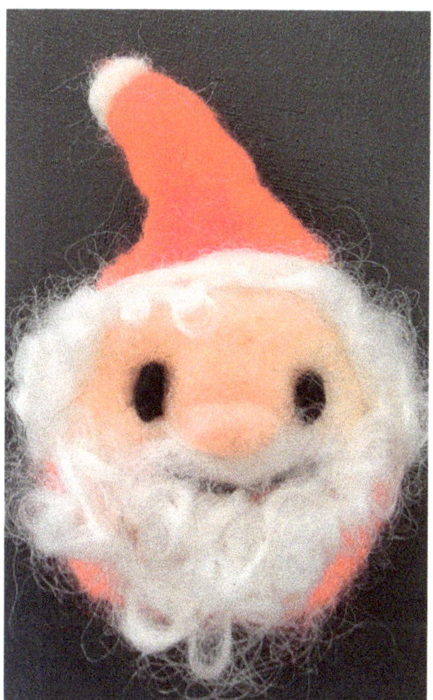

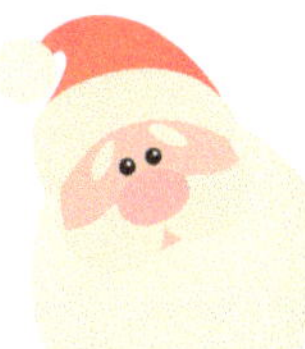

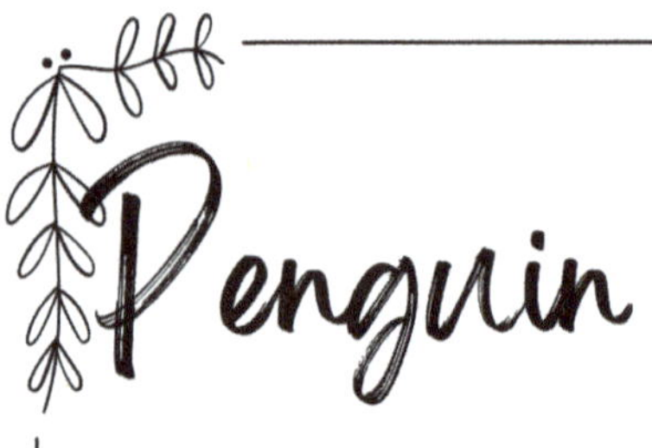

Penguin

- .5 oz Wool ball
- Small amounts: Black, red, green, white
- small round dowel

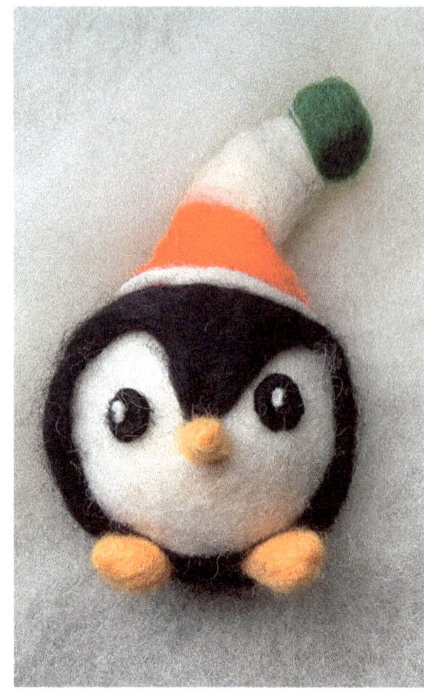

Making this adorable little fellow is fun and easy! Use your imagination to give him/her different types of hats.

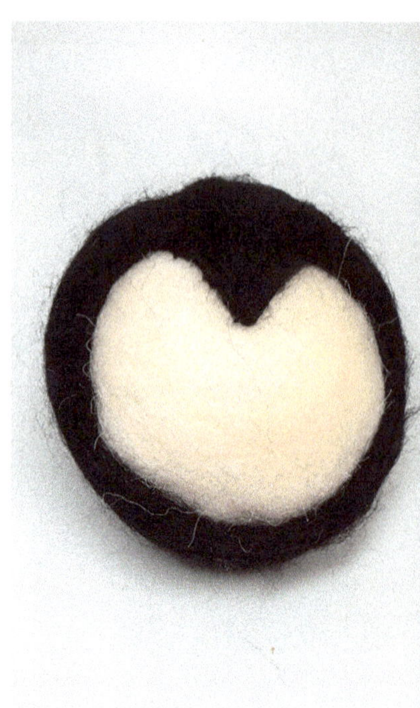

Using black wool (top or batt work equally well here), wrap around the ball leaving the front open, similar to a heart shape. Pull down a small peak from the black wool and felt down.

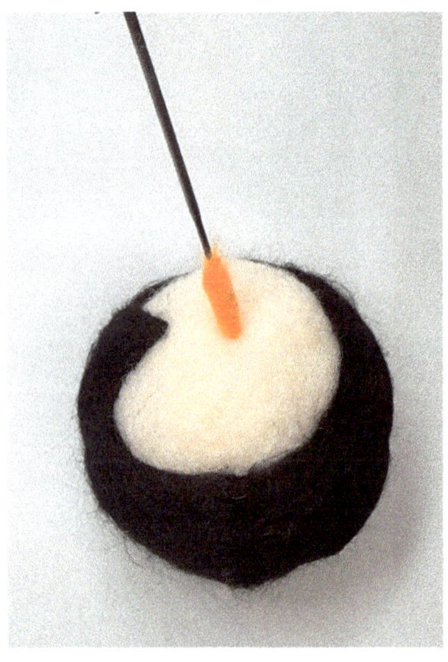

Roll orange wool around the end of your needle. Place the needle in the middle of the face. Using another needle, go around the bottom edge of the beak. Slide beak off needle and finish felting.

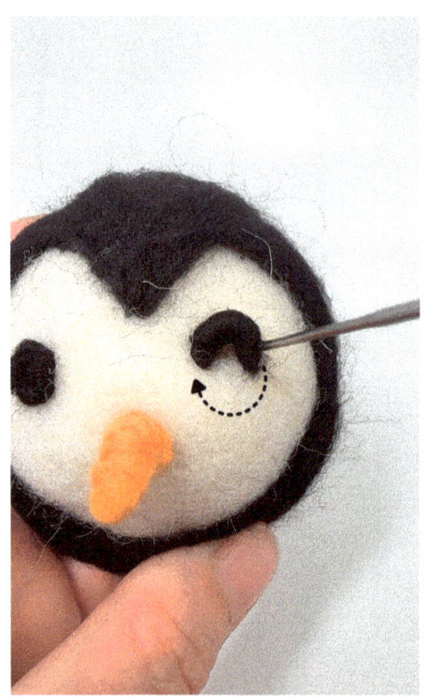

Make the eyes by rolling black on your needle, insert needle into the area you want the inside edge of the eye to be, felt. twist the eye roll into a circle, felt.

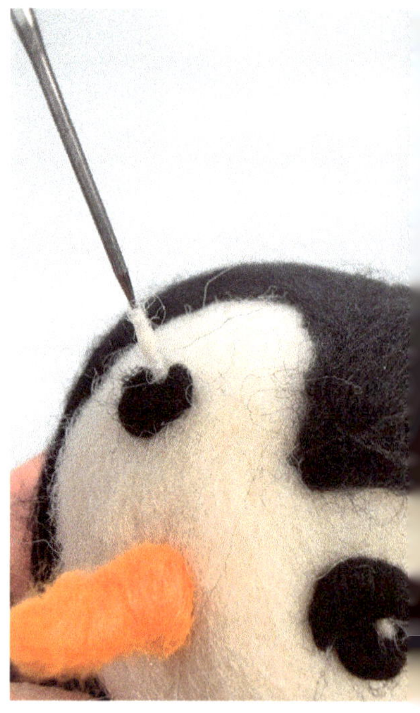

Add a tiny, white reflection spot into the corner of each eye by rolling a few strands of white onto the needle and felting directly onto the eye.

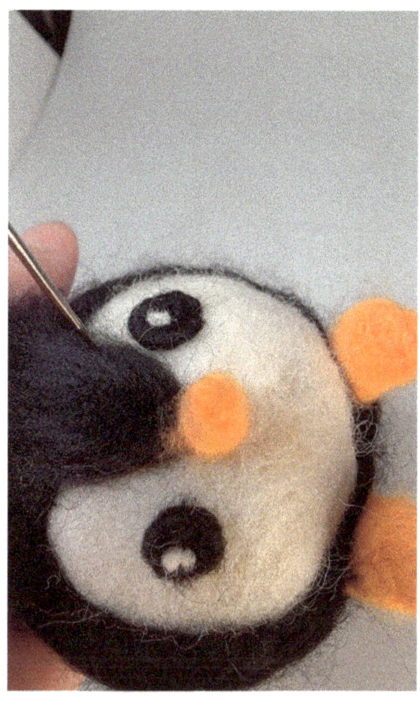

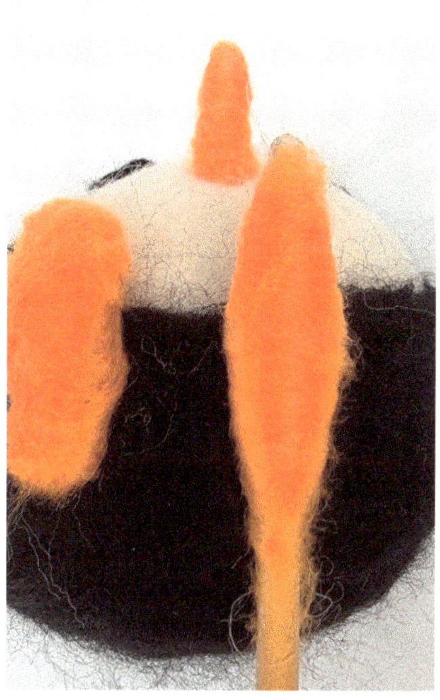

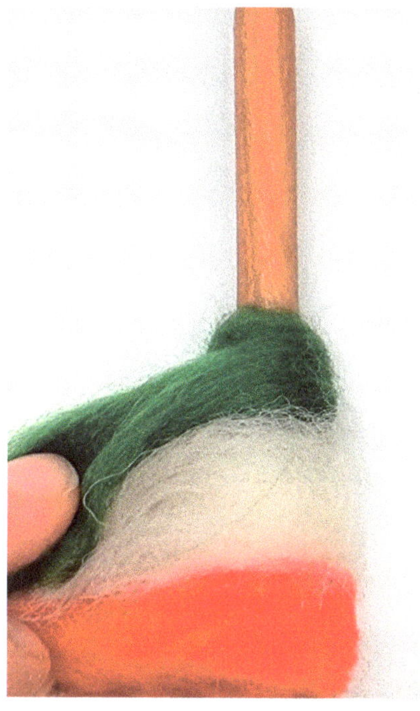

Add black wool above the beak area that flows towards the top of the head, felt down.

To form the feet, wrap a small stick with orange wool as shown. Carefully place the felted feet at the bottom and slide off the stick. Felt firmly to secure.

Create a tri-colored hat by placing different colors next to each other, then using a medium sized stick/dowel, tightly roll to the desired thickness.

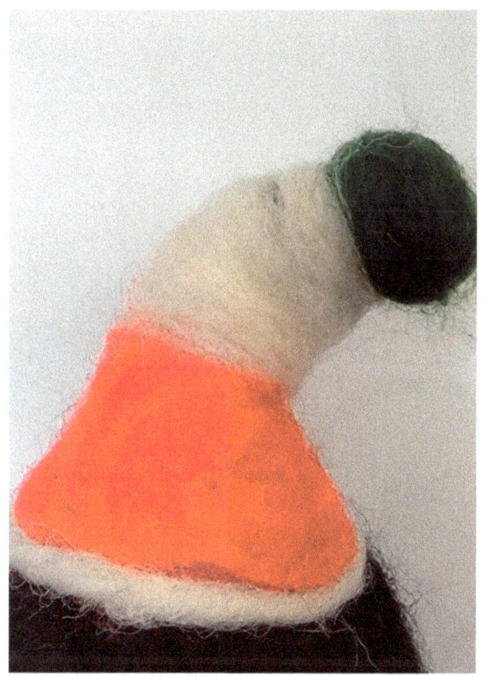

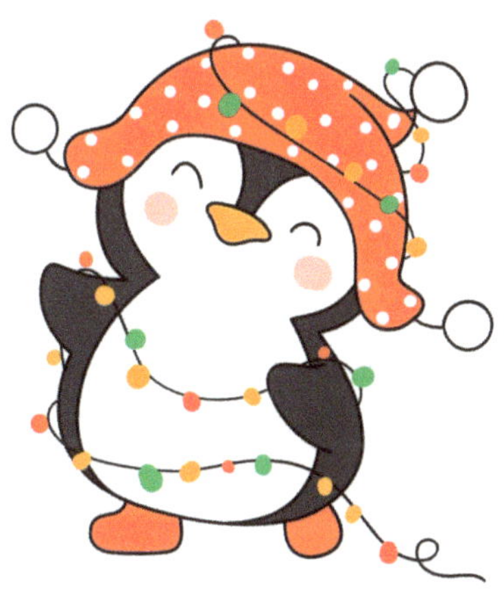

Place the hat on his head and felt down around the edge. Next, wrap additional wool around the bottom to get a fuller look. Felt down. Finally, add a thin piece of white wool to the bottom edge and felt down.

Patterns for Balls

.5 oz, 14g

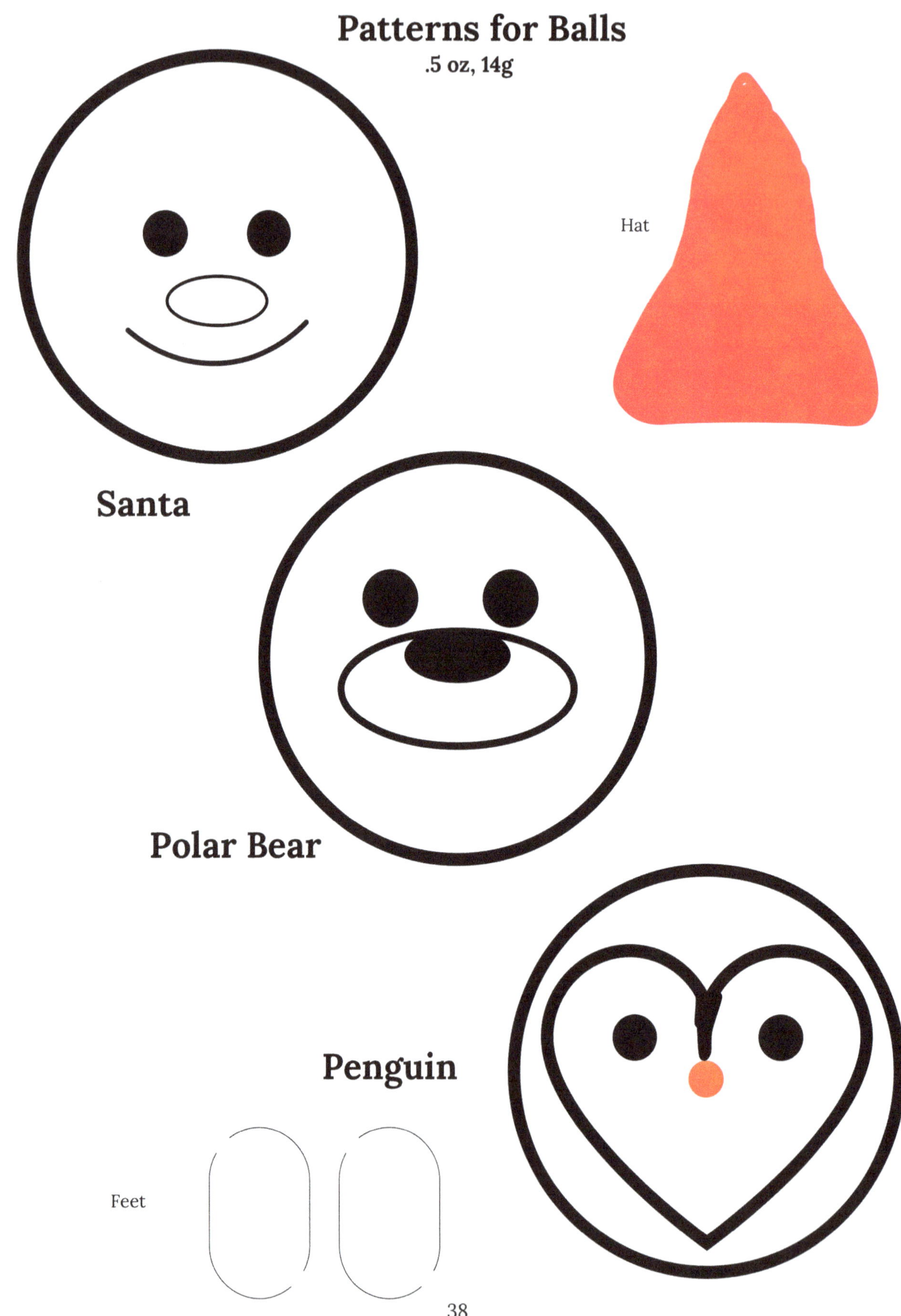

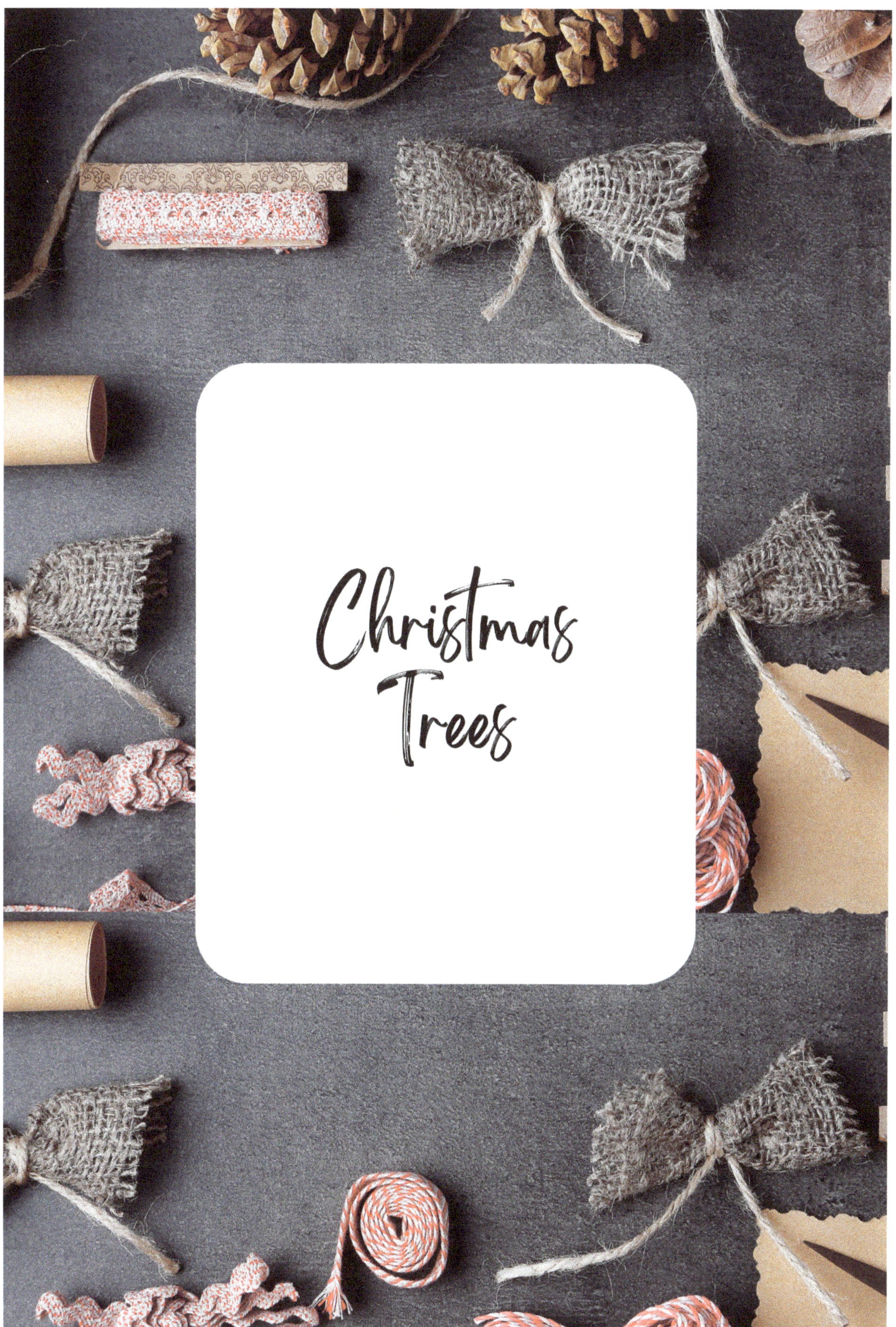

Christmas
Trees

Christmas Trees

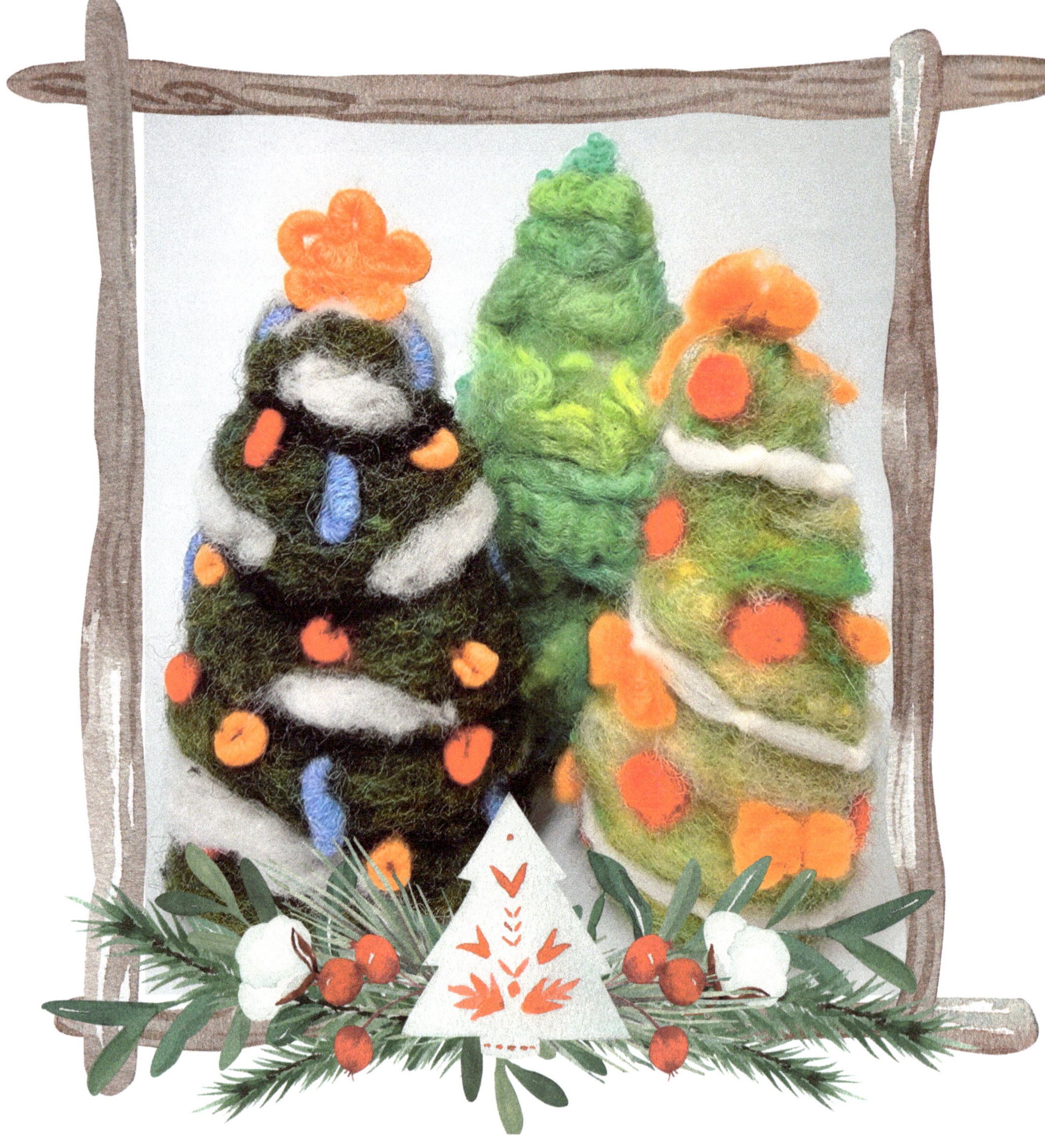

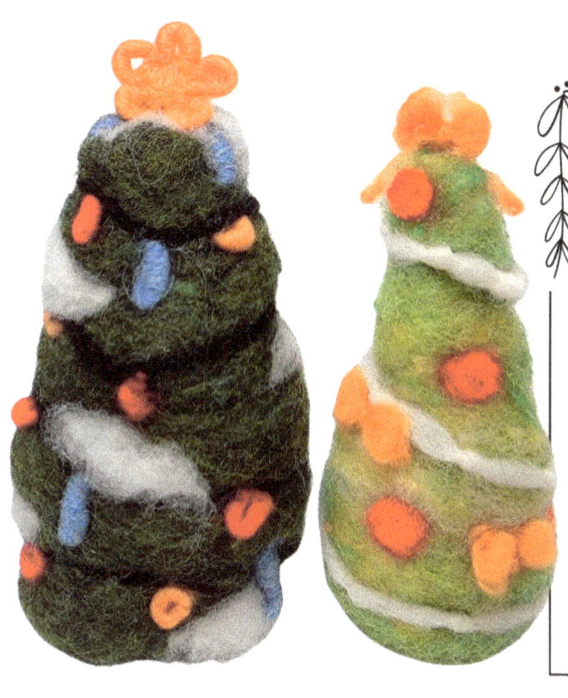

Christmas Tree

- .5 oz (14g) core wool or natural batt
- .25 oz (7g) green batt or top
- small amounts batt or top: yellow, red, blue, white, black
- Optional: Green locks

TIPS: I like to use natural batt as a core because it's so much cheaper than dyed. However, you can use green as a base if you want.

There are several ways to make a tree base. You can hand roll and fold or you can roll on a stick and add a bottom base. You choose the method you like best.

Method 1: Hand Roll

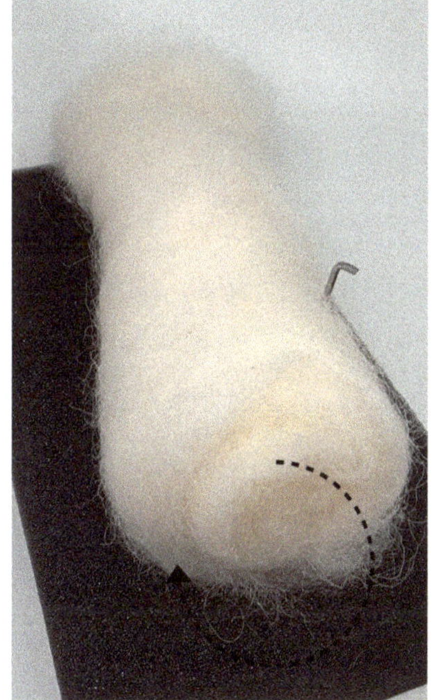

Tightly roll a 15" long piece of batt/core (38cm) and felt.

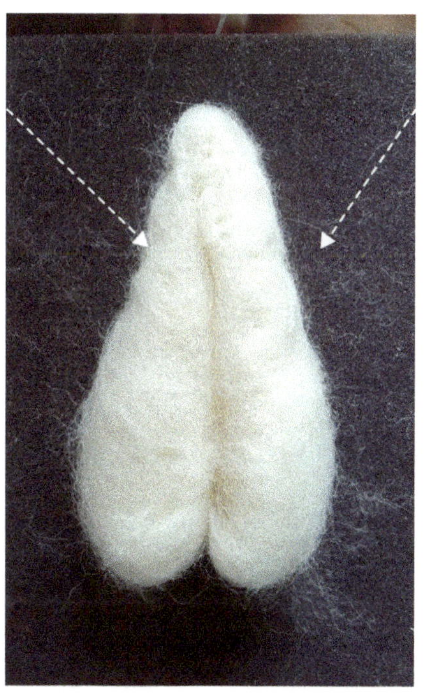

Fold the roll in half, pinch the top and then felt the top into a point. Felt around the bottom and make sure the tree is secure in its shape. Don't felt the tree too firmly though, it needs a soft look.

Method 2: Stick Roll

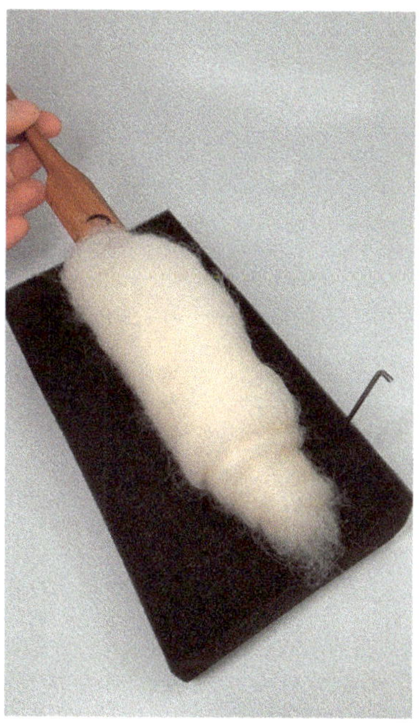

For a tree with the stick roll method, tightly wind the batt around a medium sized dowel or use the tool (see resources). Roll so that the top is thicker than the bottom. Felt carefully around the edges while it's still on the stick.

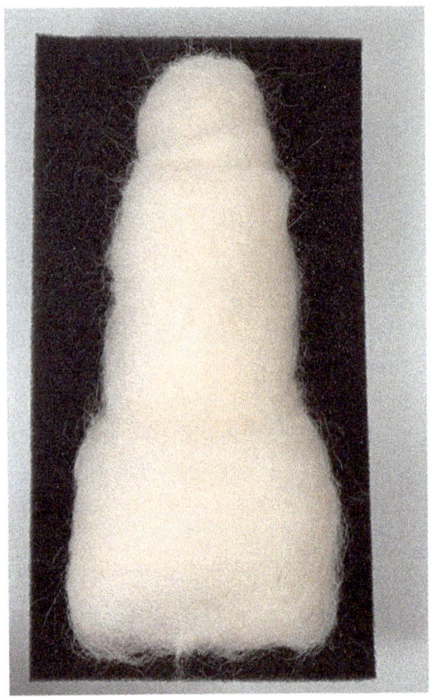

Slide off the stick and add a piece of batt to the bottom to fill the tree out and felt.

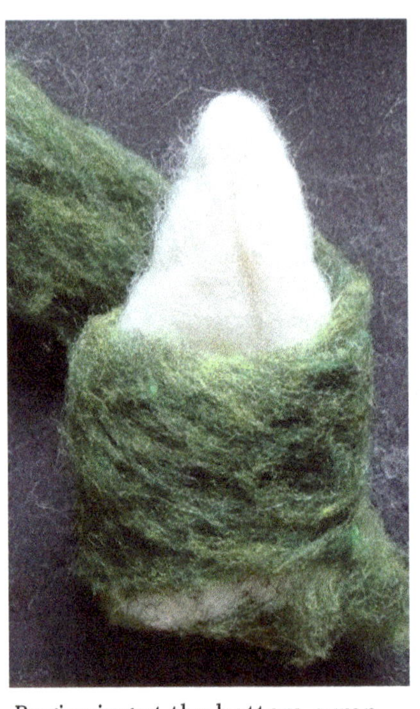

Beginning at the bottom, wrap the tree in green batt. Felt. Do not felt to firmly, you want a softer look.

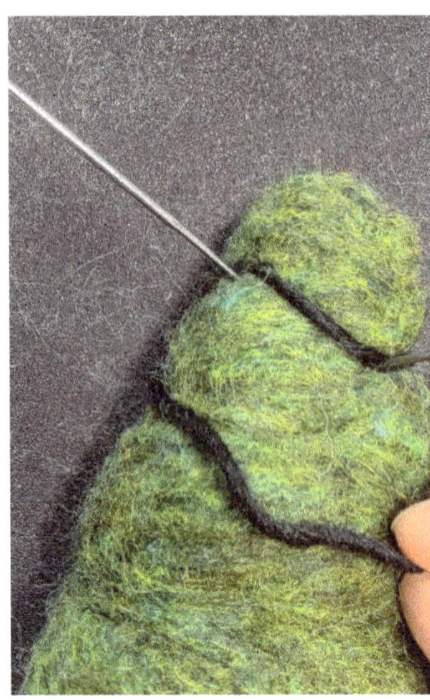

To make the light strings, use black strands. Anchor with a needle then use your fingers to twist until the strands become tight. Felt down as you hold them in place. Continue down the tree at an angle.

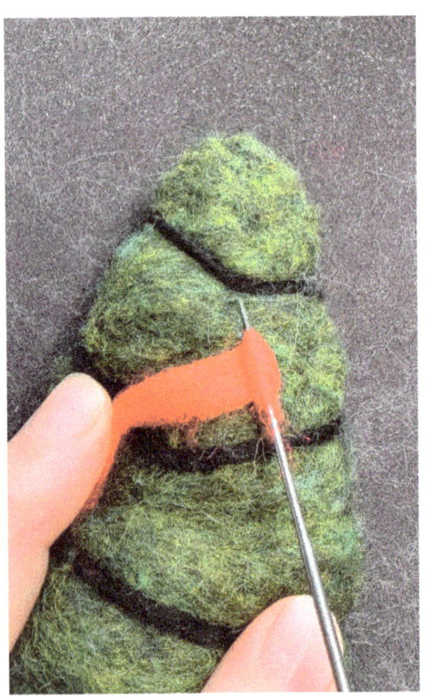

To make the bulbs or balls, simply roll wool on the end of your needle, slide off and felt directly onto the project. Use your imagination and colors that make you happy!

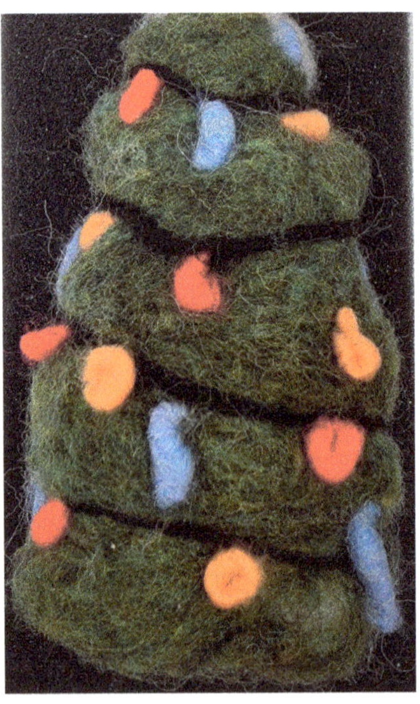

For bulbs, leave as ovals . For ornament/balls, twist a longer bulb into a circle and felt directly onto the tree.

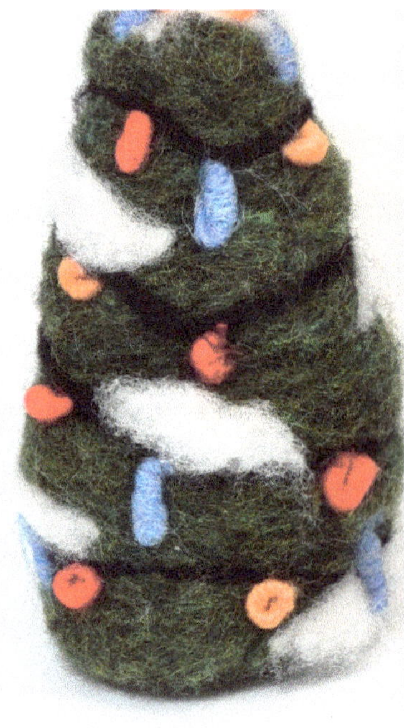

Add snow to the tree by gently layering on fluffy bits of white wool and gently felt.

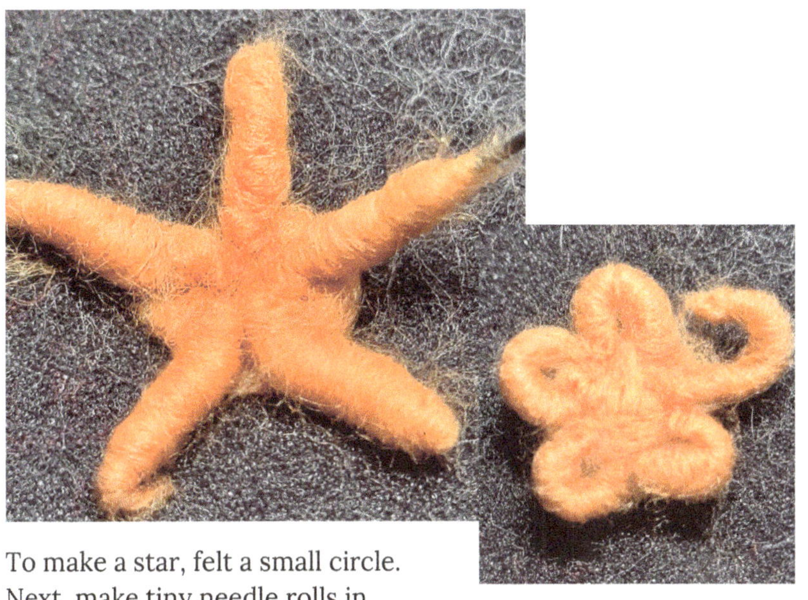

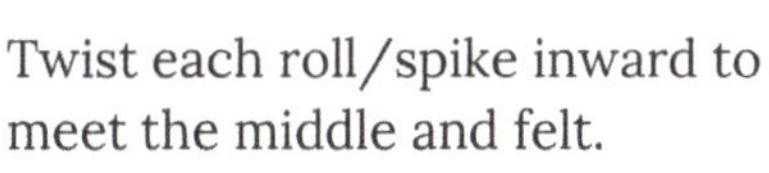

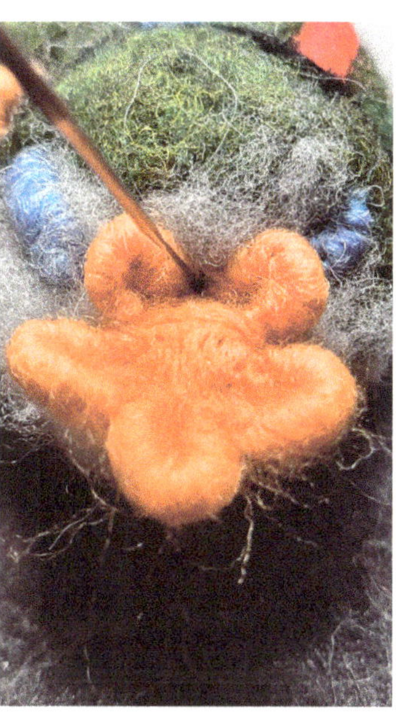

To make a star, felt a small circle. Next, make tiny needle rolls in yellow/orange and felt each one to the middle of the circle. Felt carefully to make sure nothing unravels.

Twist each roll/spike inward to meet the middle and felt.

Felt the bottom of the star to the top of the tree.

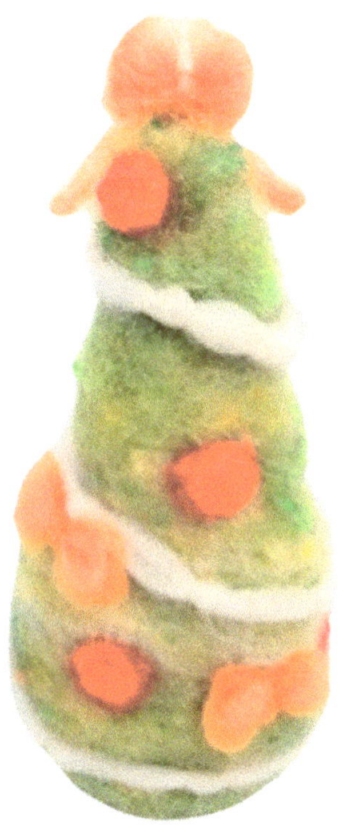

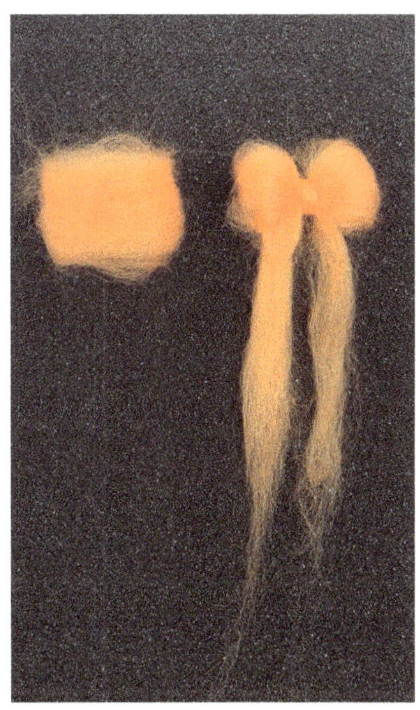

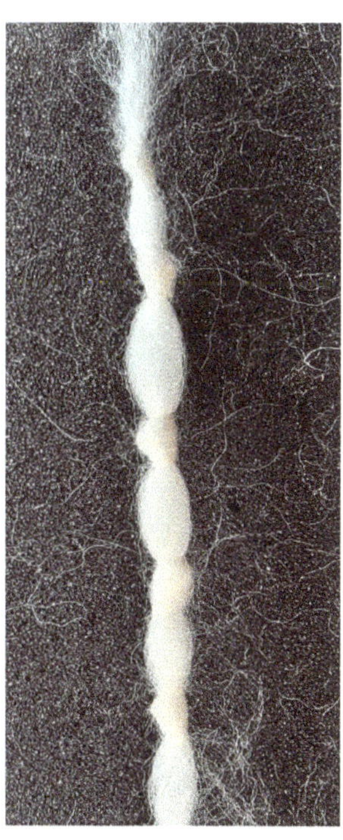

To make this tree, use a light green batt. Wrap with batt and then make red balls as above.

To make bows, simply twist a small amount of orange/yellow around your finger. Slide off then tie a piece around the middle.

To make "popcorn" garland, use a long piece of white (top is best) and tie knots all along the length. Twist this around the tree and felt gently.

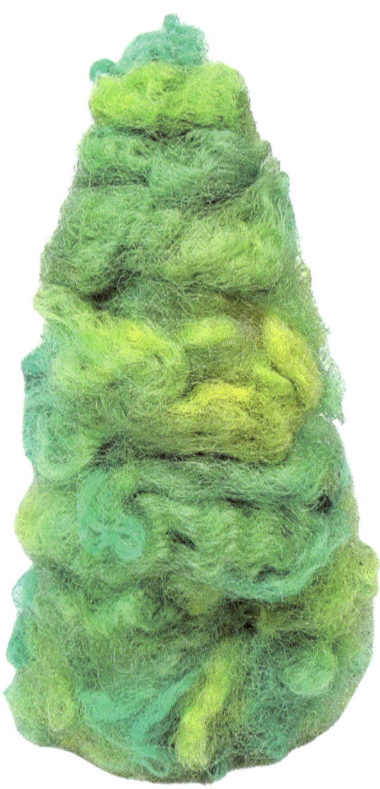

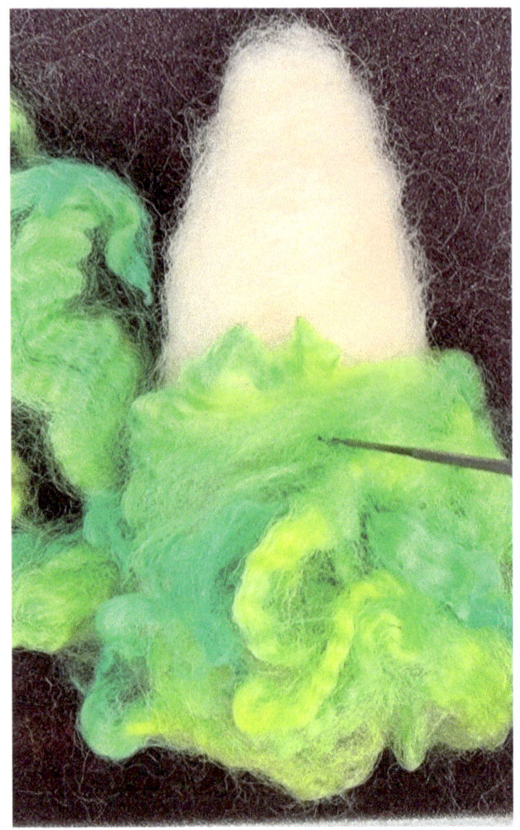

This is a fun looking tree that is made with dyed locks. The beauty of this tree is that it looks great, even without decoration. You can buy green locks or you can dye your own.

Twirl the locks around the base of the tree, lightly felting as you go. It's so easy!

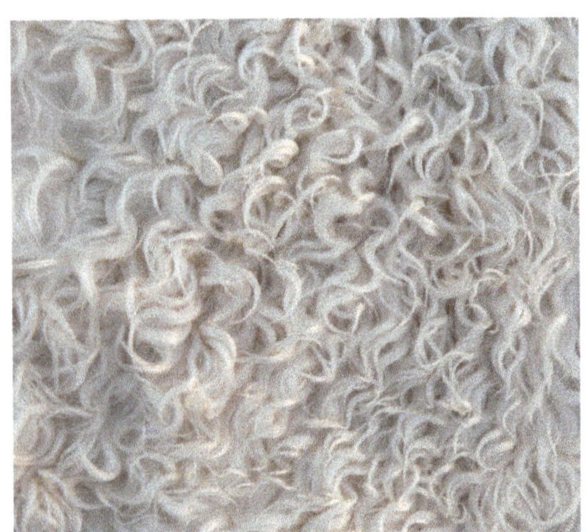

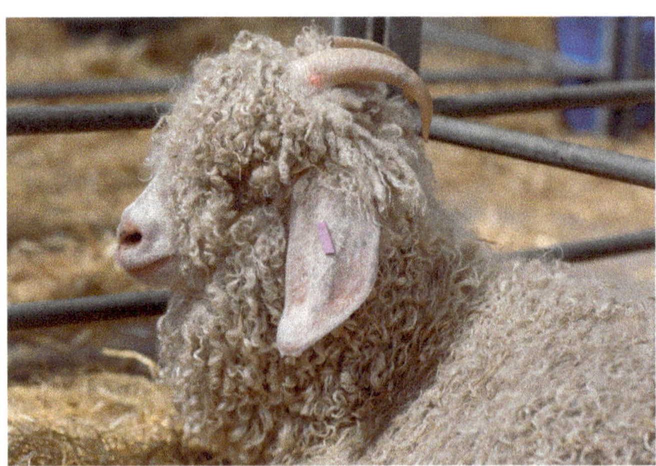

Locks are the uncombed coat of curly-coated breeds of both sheep and goats.

Buy them online buy searching for "sheep locks or goat locks".

Curly locks are a huge favorite among needle felters!

Christmas Tree

.5 oz, 14g

Tree Star

Tip to tip:
2" (5cm)

fold points into
cirlce and felt

Top 1.5" (3.81cm)

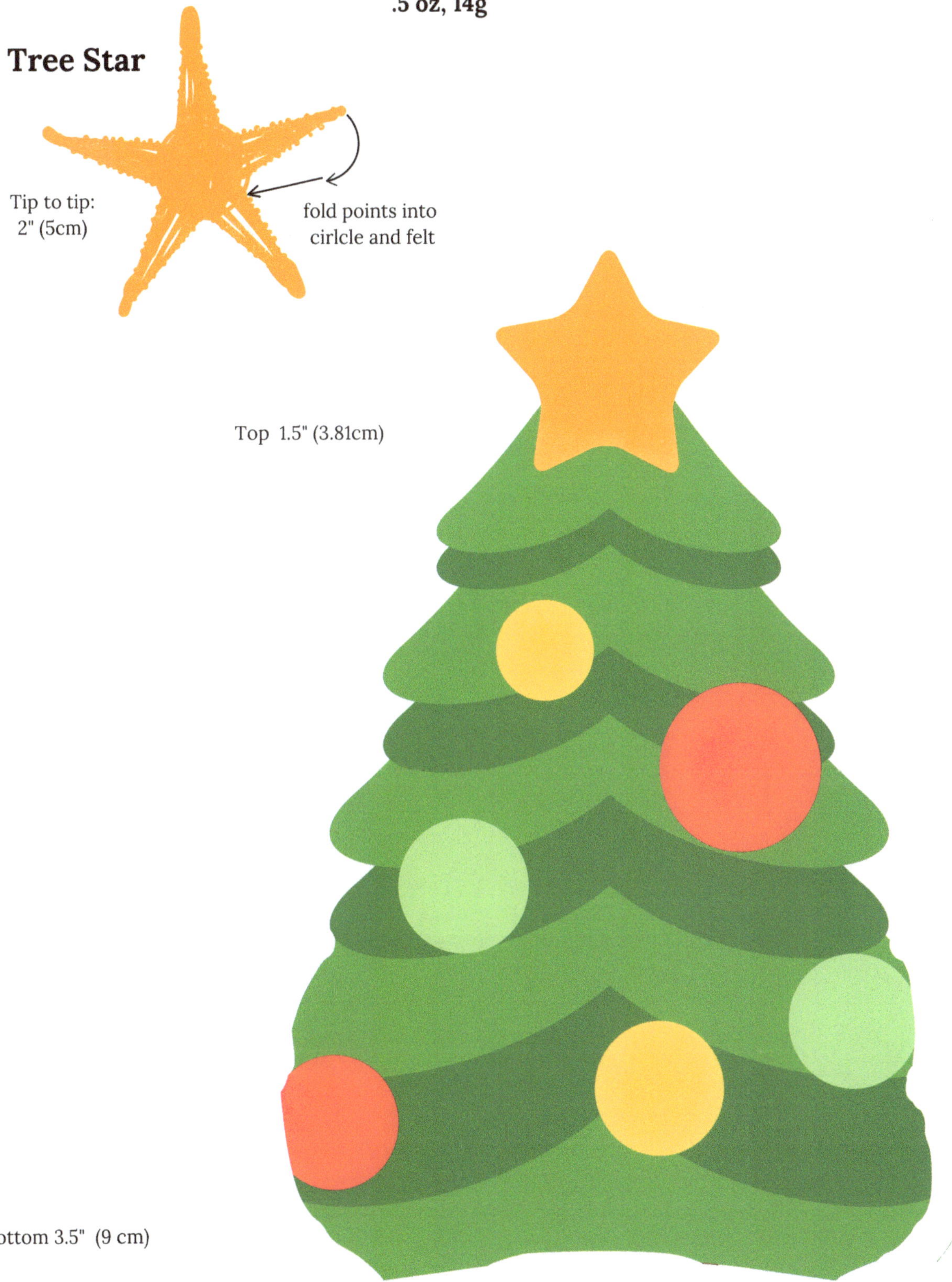

Bottom 3.5" (9 cm)

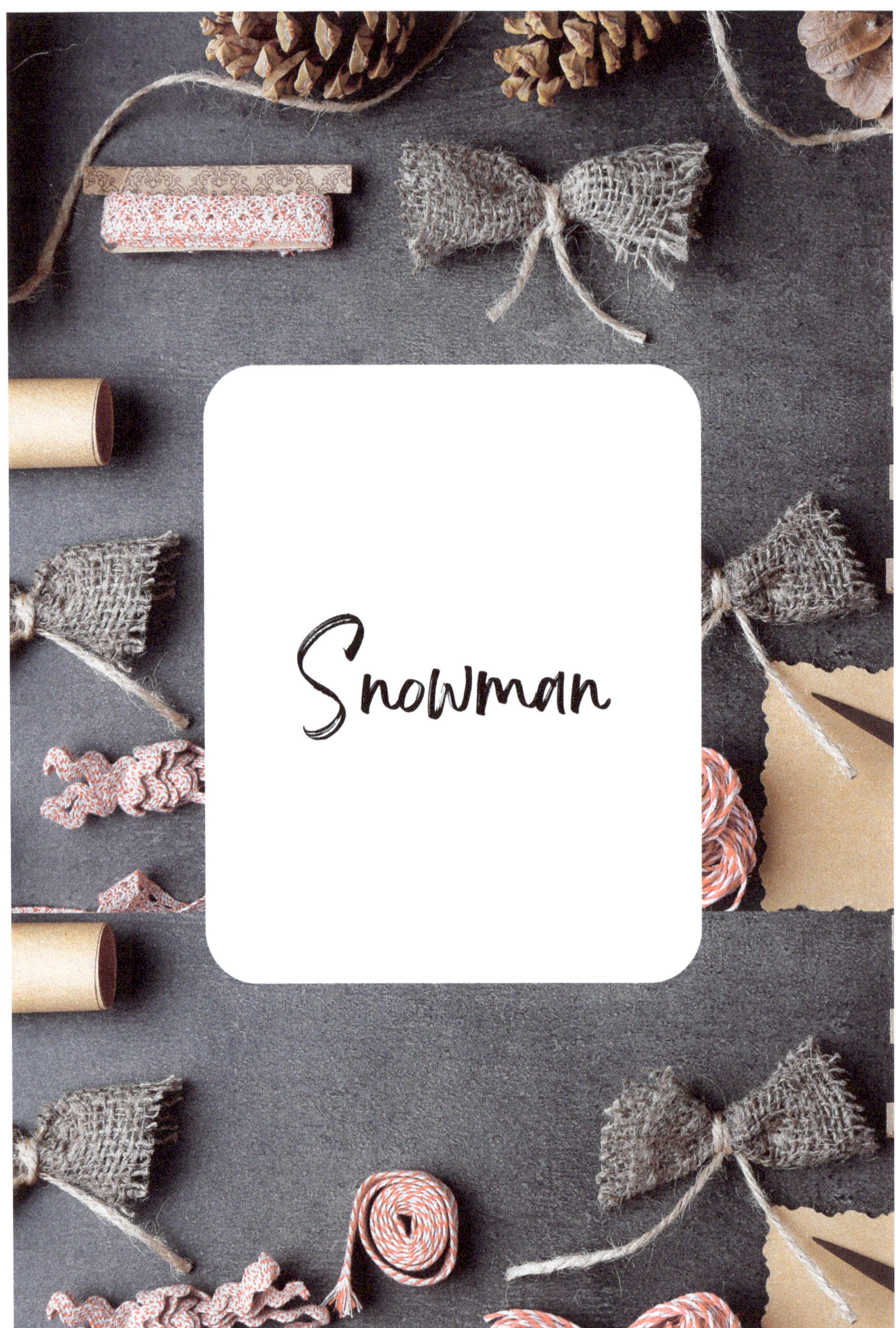

Snowman

Snowman

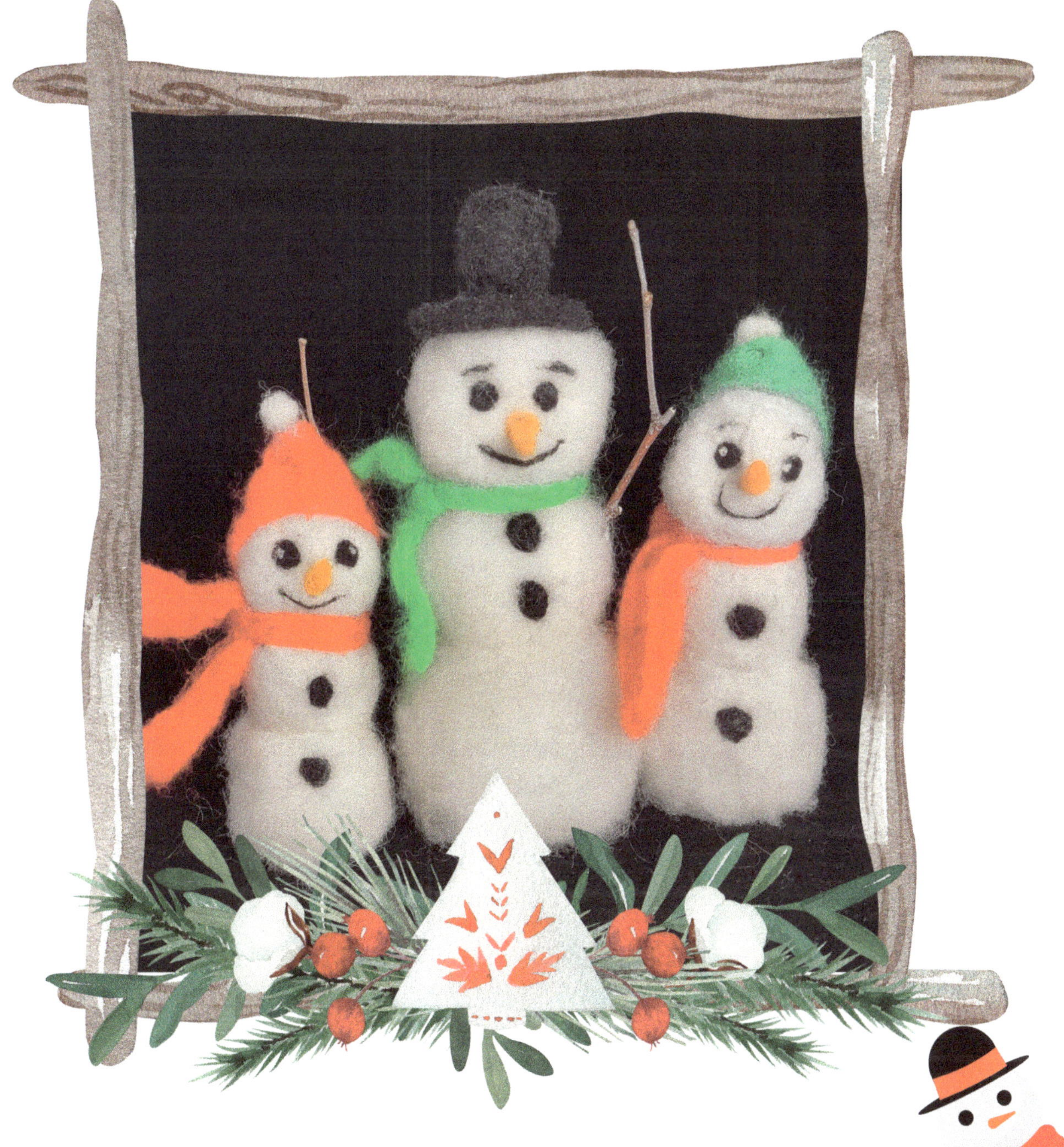

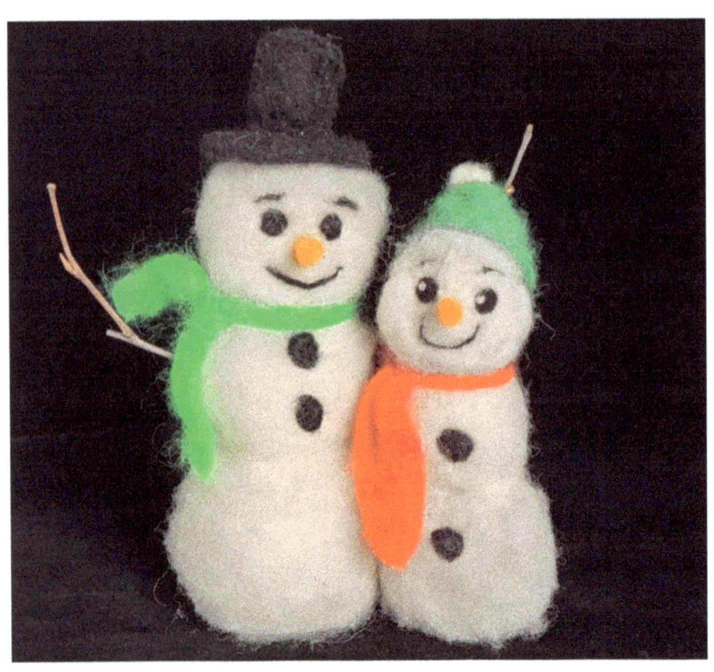

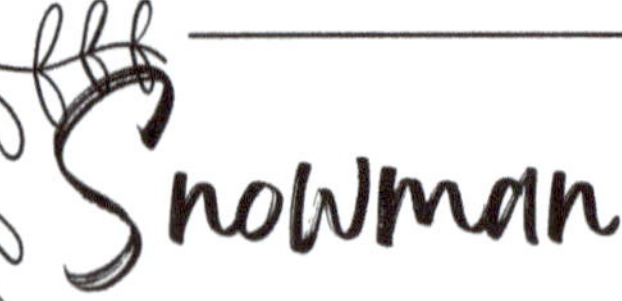

Snowman

- Body/snowballs: Batt, undyed/white (core wool) .5 oz / 14g
- Hat/Scarf: Batt or roving, any color - under .25oz
- Small amounts:
- Top: black, under .25 oz
- Batt: orange- under .25 oz
- **Optional**: Small twigs for arms
- Pom Poms for eyes and buttons, various sizes (check on Amazon or local craft stores)

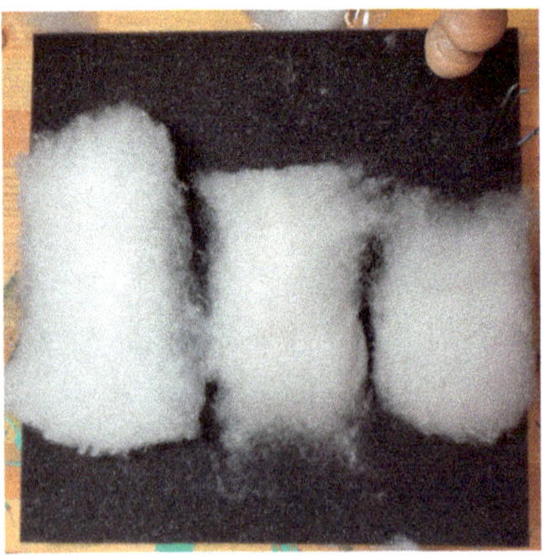

Measure out 3 pieces of batt:
bottom: 6" x 3", middle: 5" x 3" head: 4" x 3"
(cm - bottom: 15.24 x 7.67, middle: 12.7 x 7.67, head:10.16 x 7.67)

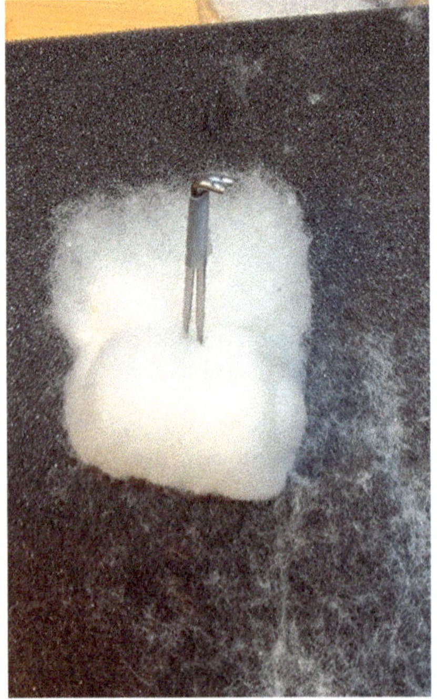

Begin by folding the batt in half and then tightly rolling up from the bottom, felting after every turn.
Alternatively, you can also use the guide on ornament balls and use the stick/roll method to make the snowballs.

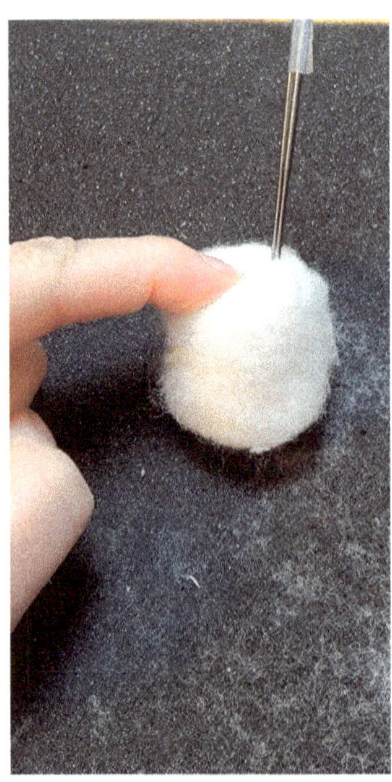

Turn the roll into a ball by rotating it and felting all around.

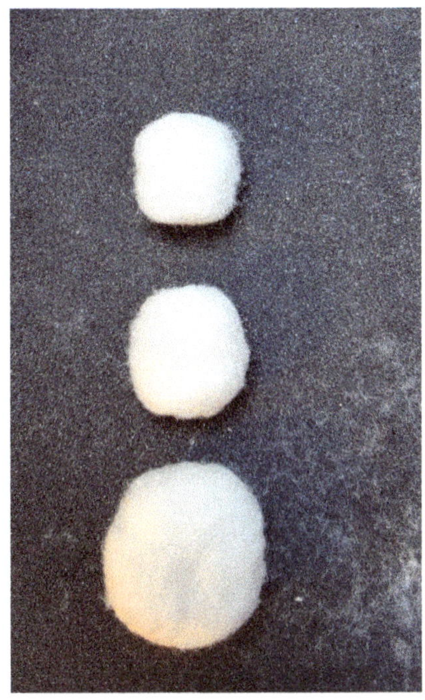

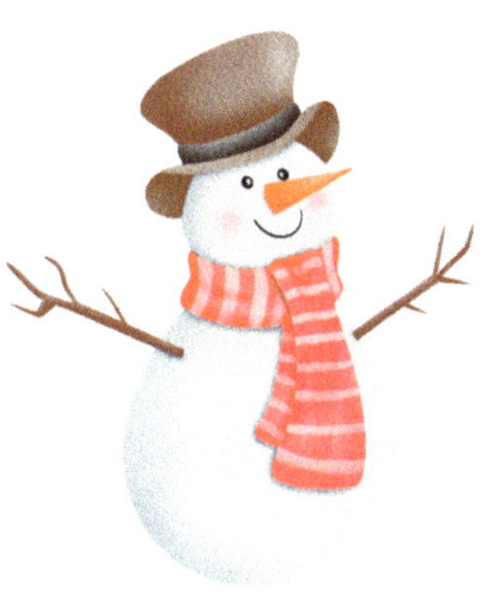

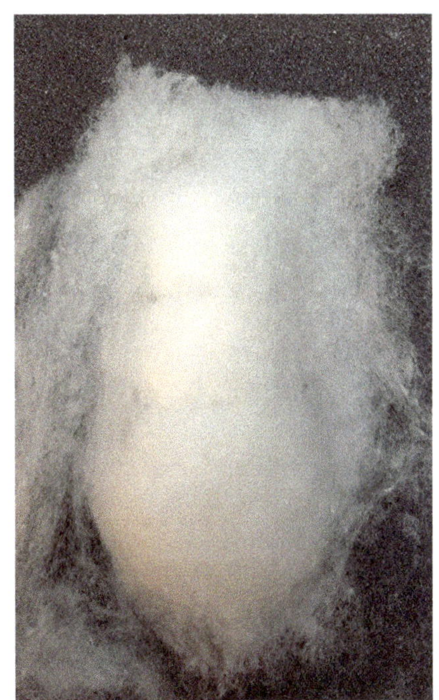

Make the three snowballs and check the sizes.
If your balls look lopsided, wrap some wool around the ball and felt.

To attach the balls together, plunge your needle through one ball and into the other while you are pressing down from the top with your fingers.

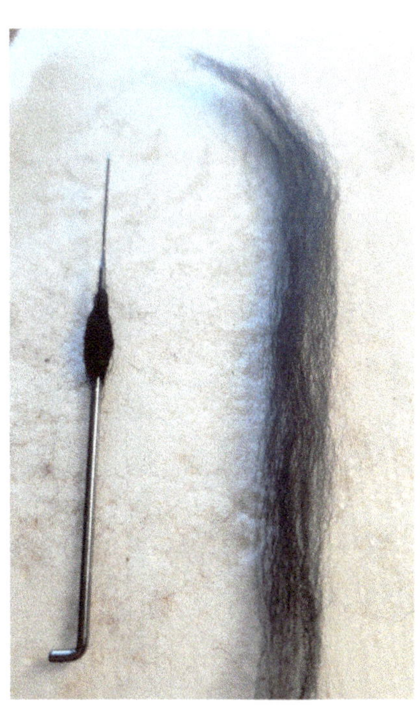

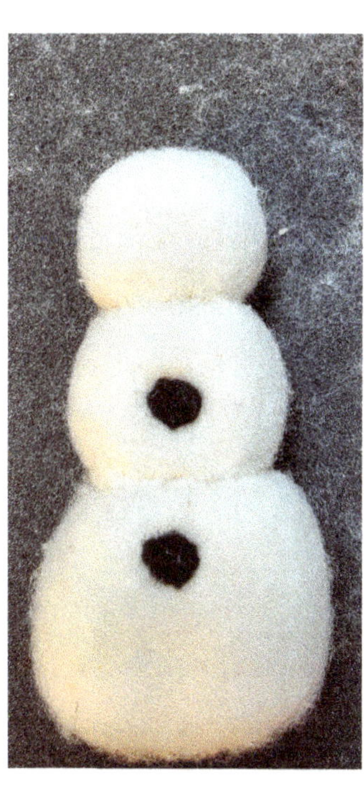

Place a thin piece of batt over the entire piece and gently felt down. This will give your snowman a full and soft, snow-like look.

To make buttons and eyes, tightly twist a small amount of wool around a needle.

Place the needle into the snowman and slide off and felt. Felt into a circular shape.

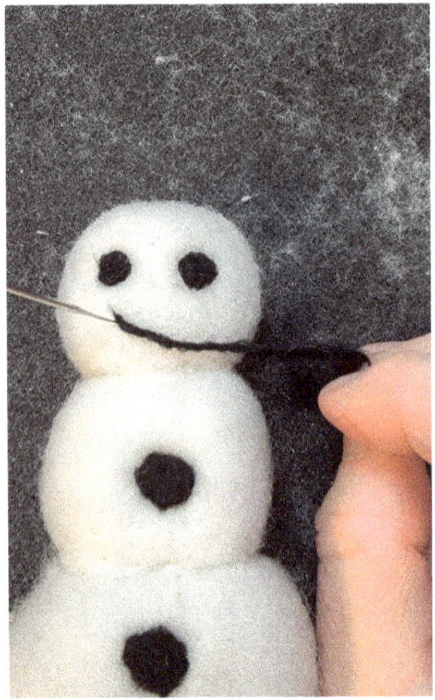

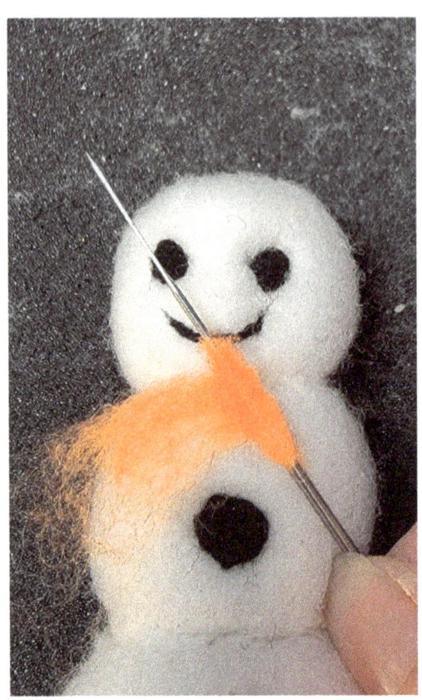

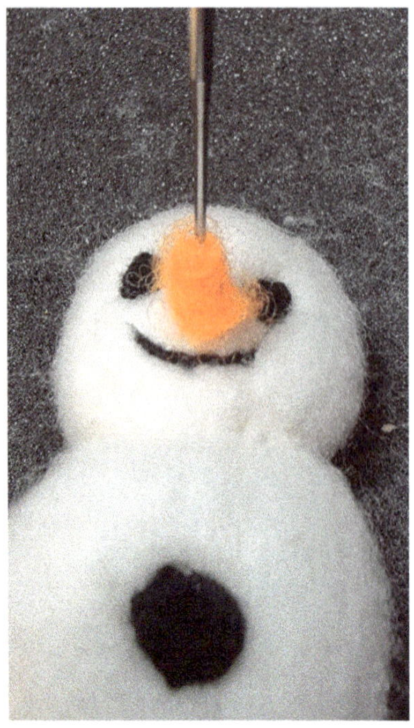

To make the mouth, use a thin piece of wool (top is best) of just a few strands and place the edge of the mouth with a needle and felt down. Twist as you felt and continue following the mouth line and felt GENTLY.

To make a carrot nose, tightly wrap a small bit of orange wool around a needle.

Place the needle in the proper position on the face. Using another needle, felt around the edges to attach. Finally, gently felt the top part of the carrot as well. Then slide the felted nose off the needle.

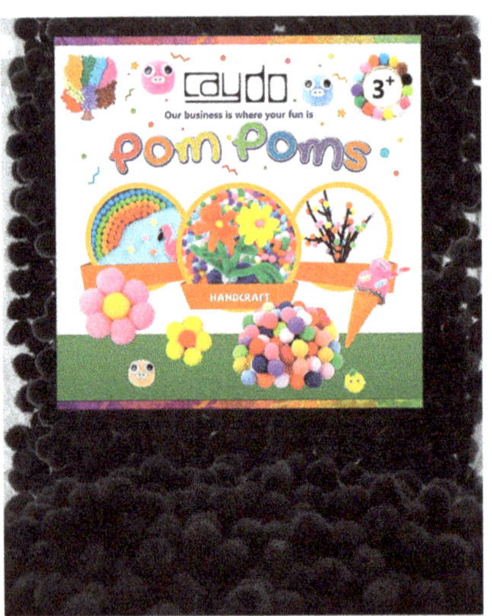

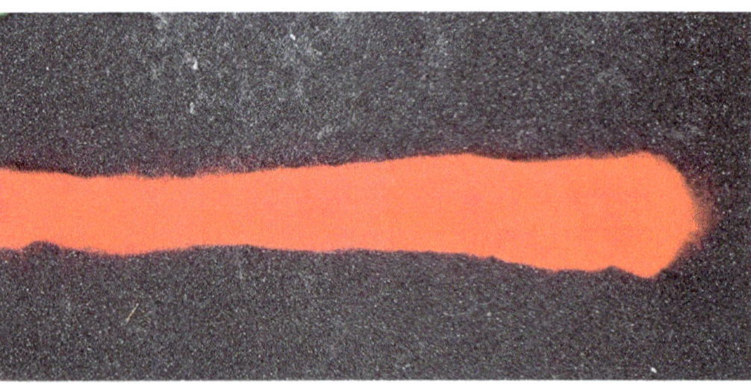

As an easy, fast alternative to making buttons and eyes, you can purchase tiny pom poms from Amazon or any craft store. They can be glued on (carefully) with a tiny amount of hot glue.

To measure the scarf, use a measuring tape to wrap around the neck. Add 1" of height and 1" of width (for shrinkage). Mark off these measurements with wool and then felt. Make sure to make the edges smooth. Wrap around his neck and tie.

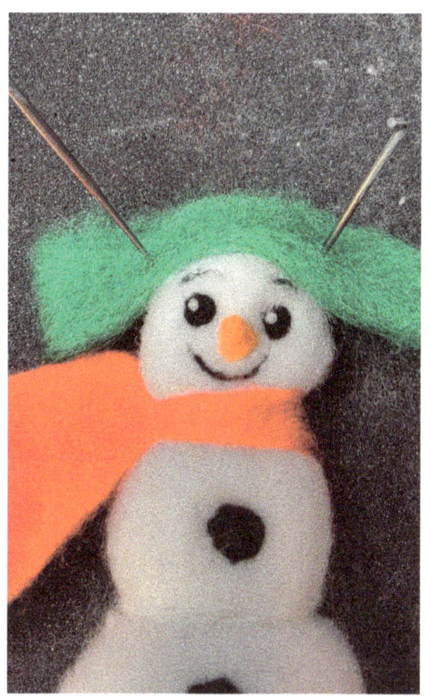

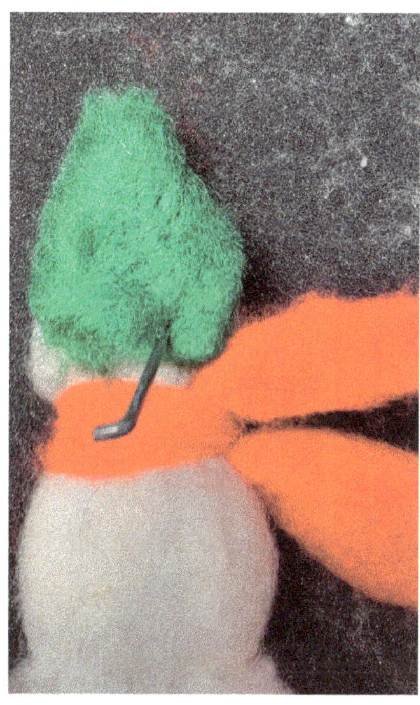

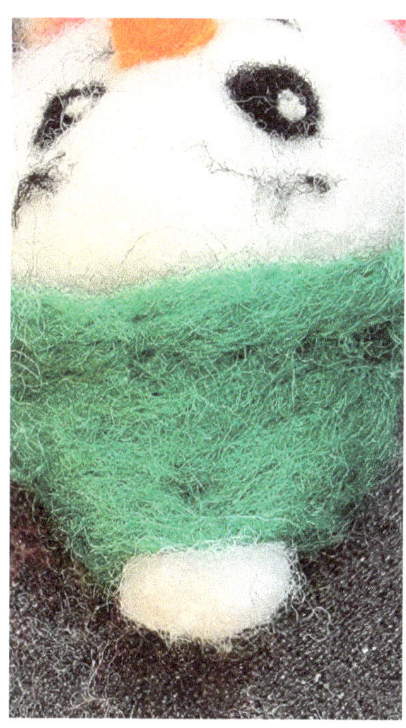

For a simple hat, use the measuring tape to wrap around his head, then add 1" to the height and width. Measure out wool to fit then felt on the pad. Transfer to the head as shown. Felt down on the forehead.

Turn the snowman over and wrap the hat so that it folds over the back and felt down.

Make a white pom as you did for the buttons/eyes and attach to the top of the hat. Add small white reflection spots and eyesbrows if desired.

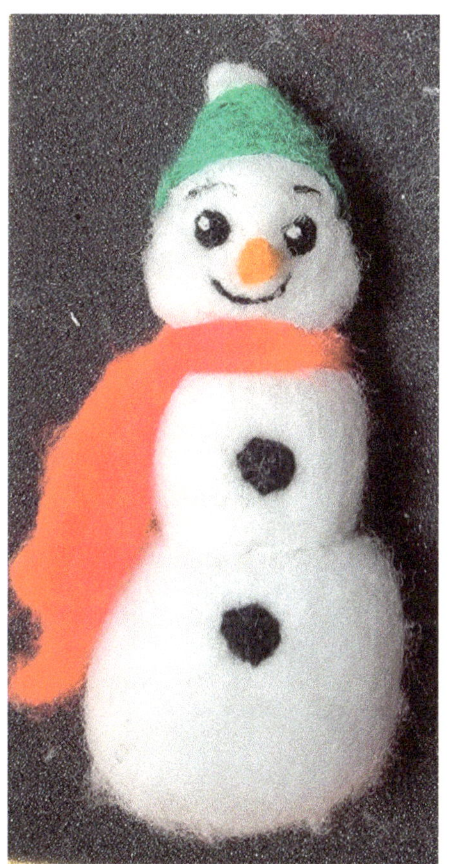

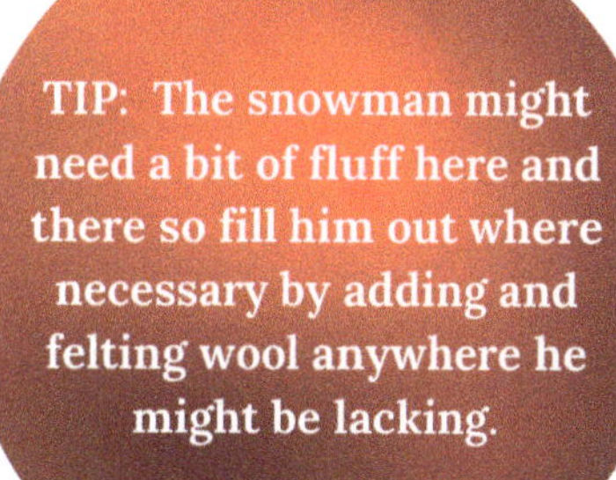

Top hat

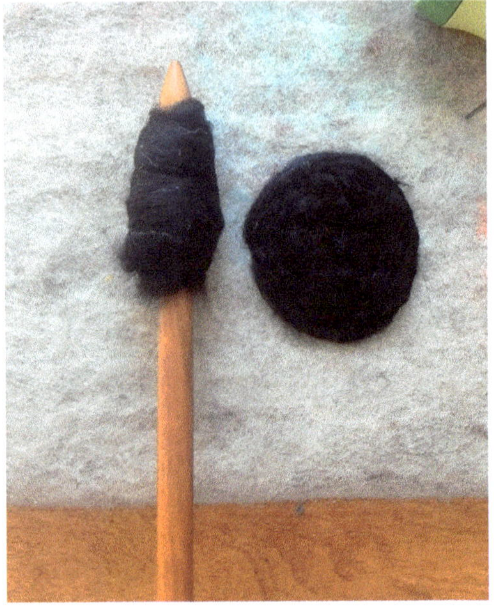

For a top hat, felt a small circle in black and check the measurements against his head as you go. Roll a black cylinder on a stick.

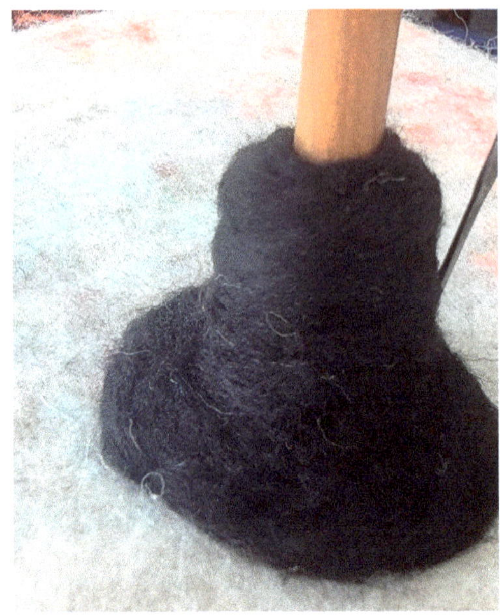

Place the cylinder/stick directly onto the circle and felt the cylinder to the circle. Make sure and felt around the top part of the cylinder as well, to make it firm. Place onto his head and felt firmly.

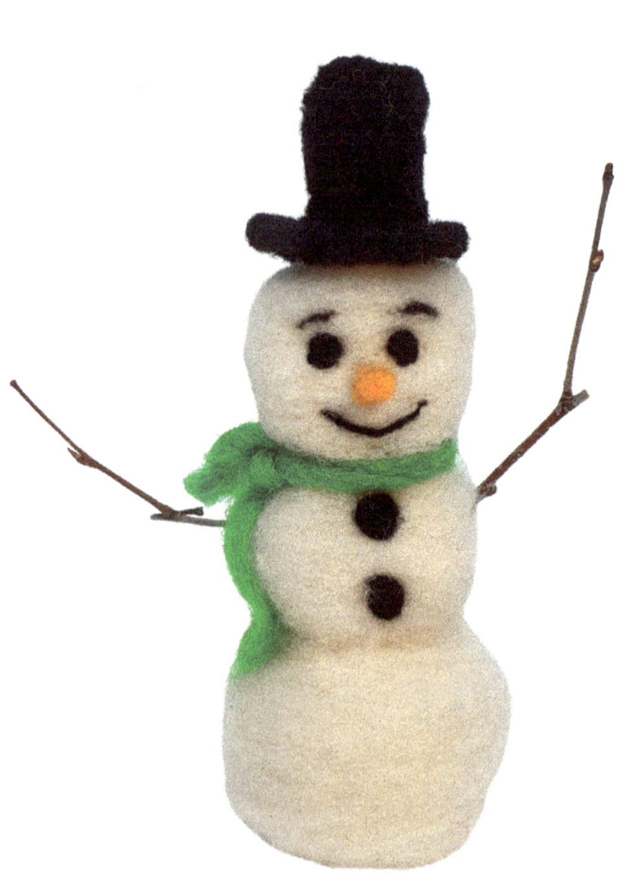

Twig Arms

If you'd like to add stick arms, make a small indentation with your needle at the arm insertion site then add a dab of hot glue and quickly glue in the stick. If any glue shows, simply cover with a bit of wool and felt gently.

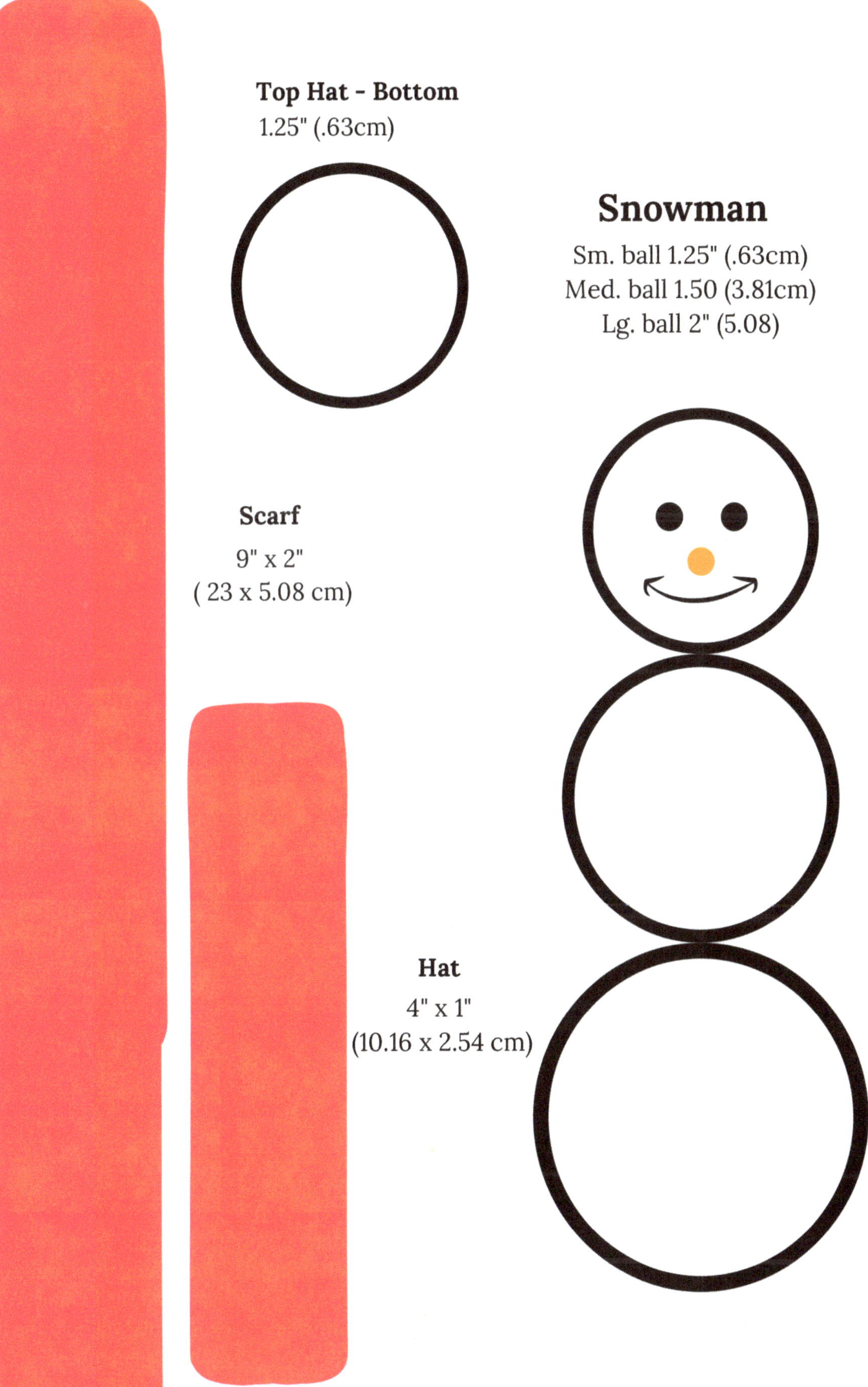

Top Hat - Bottom
1.25" (.63cm)

Snowman

Sm. ball 1.25" (.63cm)
Med. ball 1.50 (3.81cm)
Lg. ball 2" (5.08)

Scarf

9" x 2"
(23 x 5.08 cm)

Hat
4" x 1"
(10.16 x 2.54 cm)

Adding Hangers

Adding hangers to your ornaments is easy! You can use ribbon, twine, or even braided wool! Use what suits your project best.

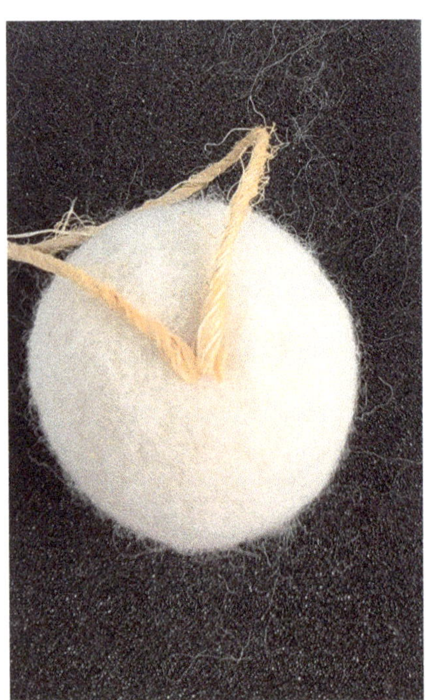

Place ribbon or twine in the area you want the hanger.

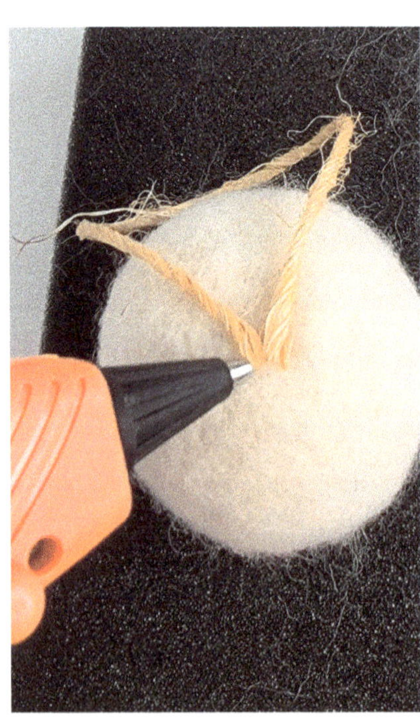

OPTIONAL: use just a dab of hot glue to give it extra holding power, especially if your ornament is on the heavy side. If your ornament is light, you dont have to use glue to secure.

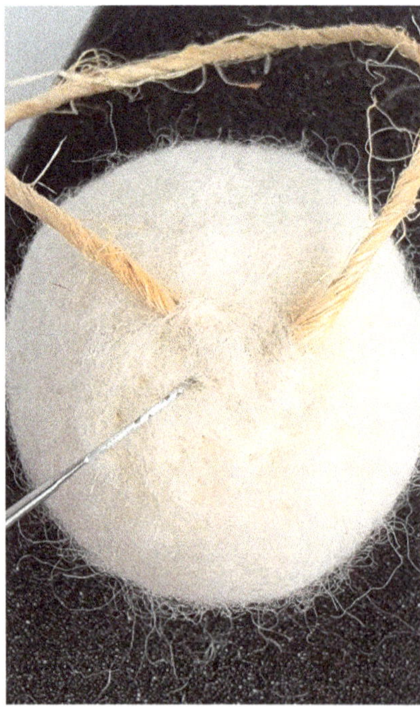

Cover the hanger with matching wool and carefully felt around the hanger. Felt firmly and this will hold the hanger to the ornament.

Resources

Visit NatureCrafty.com for updated clickable links

USA

Living Felt
livingfelt.com
Large variety of quality wool sourced from US farms. Wonderful batts. Eco-friendly

Sarafina Fiber Art
sarafinafiberart.com
Complete line of quality fiber and supplies along with great kits and tutorials. I love their roving!

Grey Fox Felting
greyfoxfelting.com
Great selection of hard-to-find colors, good prices.

Big Sky Fiber Arts
bigskyfiberarts.com
My favorite shop for a huge variety of animal colors.

Felted Sky
Feltedsky.com
High quality batts in an astounding number of shades. They sell down to .25 oz if you only need a bit.

The Woolery
woolery.com
Huge variety of fibers, including vegan. Great selection of tools and carders.

The Felted Ewe
thefeltedewe.com
Good color selection of all types of roving and batt as well as many supplies.

Canada

Fibercraft
fibrecraft.ca
An impressive array of fibers and supplies.

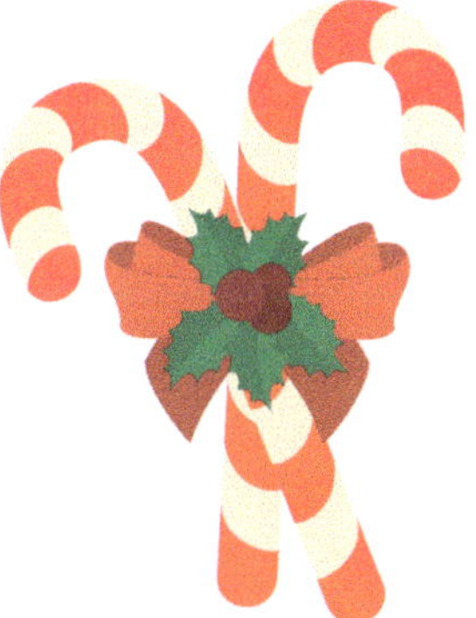

Europe

The Makerss - UK
themakerss.co.uk
Extensive needle felting wool and supplies for the UK
and abroad. Local workshops.

Sweet Pea Dolls - UK
www.sweetpeadolls.co.uk
Inspiring range of fibers, tools and kits. Worldwide shipping. Alternative fibers.

World of Wool - UK
worldofwool.co.uk
Great variety of fiber products and delivers worldwide.

Heidi feathers – UK
heidifeathers.com
Wool and is known for great needles and glass eyes.

The Dyeing House Gallery Shop - Italy
A vast assortment of very high-quality wool, sell internationally
dhgshop.it/promozioniele.php

The Wollknoll Shop - Germany
wollknol.eu.shop
Beautiful variety of colors. Tools

CreaVea - France
Creavea.com
A crafts website with a large selection of felting wool.

If you're new to needle felting, it's wise to purchase your batt from a reputable supplier specializing in felting supplies. I recommend avoiding wool from Amazon or big box retail stores, as their descriptions can often be inaccurate, and the quality is not always good.

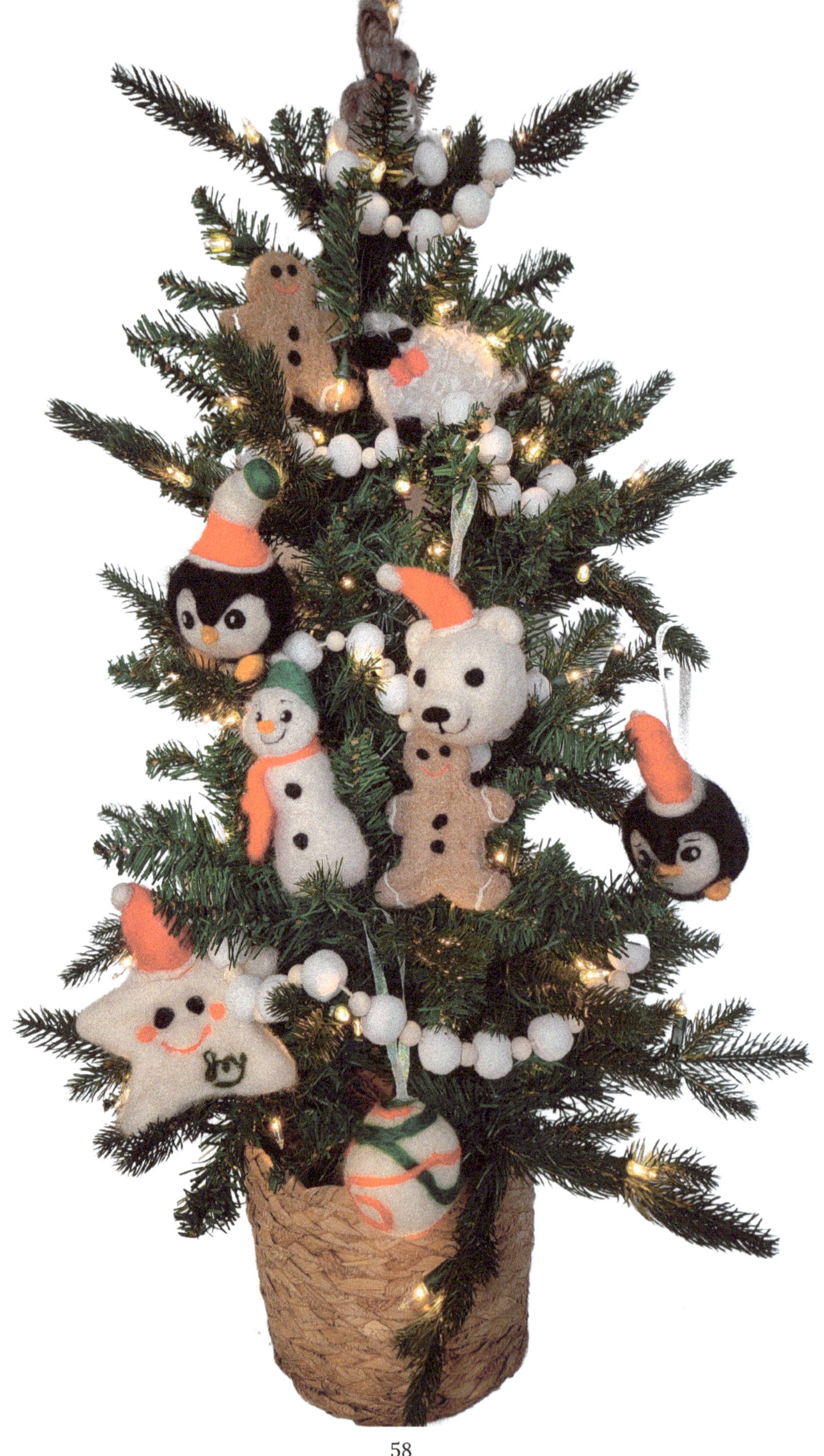